STUDIES IN PREHISTORIC CULTURES OF ANDHRA PRADESH

STUDIES IN PREHISTORIC CULTURES OF ANDHRA PRADESH

BY
D. L. N. SASTRY
Dr. M. KASTURI
G. V. RAMA KRISHNA RAO

BHARATIYA KALA PRAKASHAN
DELHI (INDIA)

First Edition : 1999

Published by **C.P. Gautam**
BHARATIYA KALA PRAKASHAN
3611/5, Narang Colony, Tri Nagar,
Delhi-110035. Phone : 7163083

ISBN : 81-86050-38-8

Laser Type Setting by
A-ONE GRAPHICS
X-4, Gali-2, Brahmapuri, Delhi-110053
Phone : 218 3470

Printed at Santosh Offset Press
40, Anand Nagar, Inderlok, Delhi
Phones : 511 6763, 511 7390

Dedicated

to

Dr. V. V. Krishna Sastry

Contents

Foreword

The present work "Studies in pre-historic Culture of Andhra Pradesh" by Shri D.L.N. Sastry is aimed at providing logical and reasonable awareness of Earth's past and the history of human life, besides a brief description of the various stages in the evolution of Man. According to Sir James Jeans, the entire solar system is as small as a particle in the total area of the universe and the knowledge so far attained is relative and limited. It is just like the extent of the brightness of a torch in an extensive area in darkness. However, from the historical facts, it is evident that philosophers like Confucius, Buddha, Lovotes, Socrates etc. tried to understand nature around us and the role of man during 2800-1600 years before present. However the scientific inquiry has been going on since Bacon during the last 300 years. Palaeolithic and post-Palaeolithic evidences in India began appearing from the last part of the 19th century. With the aid of these discoveries, the pre-historians began studying spacio-temporal aspects of stratigraphy and techno-temporal aspects with the inter-disciplinary approach for probing into the life ways of pre-historic people.

The author has successfully provided basic archaeological data fot the various evolutionary phases of Man in Andhra during the Lower, Middle, Upper and Microlithic periods of the palaeolithic age supported by illustrations. He has also classified the unpublished artefacts collected from various parts of the State since 1960 by the department.

The book also makes simple reading to understand and identify the varied tool types, the raw materials used, probable function of a tool in a given economy and the advances made in tool making techniques. The discoveries made and interpretations given for each sub period by eminent research scholars in the field are also recorded. This enables interested students in the field to take up independent study.

The author, Shri D.L.N. Sastry with his deep knowledge of pre-history rendered yeomen services in high lighting the Stone Age culture of Andhra-desa. A glance through the book reveals the pains the author has taken to bring out a work of this nature. Being a senior officer in the Department of Archaeology and Museums, with vast experience in the field of Ancient Indian History, Culture and Archaeology and scholarly background his work provides fascinating study in pre-historic archaeology. I have no doubt that this work will receive the attention of the scholarly world, students and the public at large. I whole heartedly wish that the author, Shri D.L.N. Sastry, should continue his pursuits of this sort and bring out more works on pre-history and culture of Adhra Pradesh and India.

I wish him good luck.

V. Sarma Rao, I.A.S.
Commissioner
Archaeology and Museums
Govt. of A.P., Hyderabad.

Preface

General survey on Stone age evidences has been carried out by the State Department of Archaeology and Museums, Andhra Pradesh, Hyderabad since 1960, and discovered a good number of artifacts from various sites in Andhra Pradesh. Organization of Prehistoric Gallery in Sri Sailam Pavilion, a Museum in the premises of the Directorate of Archaeology during the year, 1998 brought to public the said discoveries, however, they remained unpublished. The material selected from various sites by the department and displayed in the Plates (showcases of the Museum), forms the source material for this work, "Studies in Prehistoric Cultures of Andhra Pradesh".

Fundamental information in Earth Science, Life History and Anthropology is provided in Plates as background knowledge in brief. For a better understanding of tools, a detailed note on each artifact in Plates is also given. Some more description is provided on tools though not covered by Plates for type-sites of the Microlithic period such as Ghanpoor, Sitapalli and Chennaraopet. The aim behind this is to enable interested students to make out different pointed, edge and multipurpose tools in the assemblages of different periods of the Palaeolithic and Microlithic. Also, to get information about the nature and stage of manufacture, raw material selected, techniques applied, probable function a tool served in a given economy and the progress made. Self-explanation in Plates may enable independent study.

Brief information on the researchers made and interpretations given in the Lower, Middle, Upper and Microlithic Periods by scholars in the field is also recorded for a clear understanding.

First, I wish to express my appreciation to my colleague, Dr. M. Kasturi who extended so much co-operation in the preparation of Plates and Manuscript. Also my appreciation to Sri Ramakrishna, Technical Assistant, who associated with us in the entire work sincerely.

I am thankful to Sri N. R. V. Prasad, former Director, Department of Archaeology and Museums, Government of Andhra Pradesh, Hyderabad, for initiating me to this work.

My sincere thanks are due to Sri S. Dasarathi Chief Museum Officer, Department of Archaeology and Museums, Government of Andhra Pradesh, Hyderabad, for his expert guidance in the arrangement of Plates.

I also thank for the co-operation of my friend, Sri Jogi Naidu the present Chief Museum Officer, Department of Archaeology and Museums, Government of Andhra Pradesh, Hyderabad.

I am oblised to Sri V. Sarnia Rao, I.A.S., Commissioner, Archaeology & Museums Department, Government of Andhra Pradesh, Hyderabad for his consideration and his kind foreword.

I specially thank my daughter Dr. D. A. Padmavathi, and my son D. K. Srinivasan for taking up the editing work with so much understanding.

D. L. N. SASTRY

List of Abbreviations

AMBD	Amarabad
CRP	Chennaraopet
DPD	Dupad, Danavulapadu
DMV	Dharmavaram
DVD	Dharmapadu
GDA	Guddiveeraiah satram
GDL	Giddaluru
GDLA	Gundala
GDPA	Gondagajonnavadu
GPR	Ghanpur
INM	Inumella
IPL	Ippalapalle
IRP	Irlapadu
KDK	Kandukuru
KMK	Kamakuru
KNL	Kurnool
KDN	Konidina
MCP	Manchalakattapalle
MJR	Murtuzapur
MDR	Maddur
MRP	Marripadu
NRK	Narsimhakonda
NLR	Nellore
NDP	Nadimpalle
NGN	Nagarjunanagar
NGKD	Nagarjunakonda
PRG, PGR	Phanigiri
PVM	Polavaram
PDP	Pamidipadu
PDT	Prodduturu
RPL	Raipalle
RCM	Ramachandrapuram

RJP	Rajupalem
SGK	Singarayakonda
STP	Sitapalle
SML	Somasila
TMP	Timmalapalem
VGR	Venkatagiri
YPL	Yeparla
YLM	Yeleswaram

List of Plates*

List of Figures

* The plates and their numbers in the book exactly correspond to the show cases and their numbers in Sri Sailam Pavilion—a Museum located in the premises of the Directorate of Archaeology and Museums, Andhra Pradesh, Hyderabad.

Chapter —I

Introductory

About two million years ago climate and topological changes led to a series of great continental glaciers covering large areas of northern hemisphere with a thick sheet of ice. These two million years of expanding and contracting continental ice sheets in four spells are the Pleistocene epoch. During this epoch, there were fluctuations of the present sea level, ranging from a maximum of 200 mts, and to a minimum of 150 mts. As a result large areas of the continents were submerged and exposed. The principle effect of the advancing and receding ice-sheets (glaciers) has been to cause rapid changes of distribution in animal and plant species. Extreme climatic changes of the Pleistocene time appear to have led to relatively little extinction of animals and plants. A large number of land mammals such as Mammoths, Mastodons, Ground Sloths and Sabre-Tooth Cats became extinct in Late Pleistocene time.

Scientists basing on the evidences of fossils - the remains of ancient animals and plants, could study the kind of life existed and the changing environment of the past. They believe that the history of life is two billion years old and it is closely linked with earth sciences, which is four or five billion years old. Fortunately during the Pleistocene period in the history of life, they could observe the evolutionary sequence of man more clearly than his ancestor's in the Pre-Pleistocene period. The oldest Pleistocene men are now assigned to Genus Australopithecus. The Australopithecines were succeeded in the middle Pleistocene time, by large brained species Homo erectus i.e. so like modern man.

Man with his physical organism, is subjected to natural laws as other animals. But he is a unique social organism. Similar to bee society individuals carries out their life roles with instinctive and without coaching from their parents are other elders. For man, however, most behaviors are learned. Again man's uniqueness lies in his capacity for culture—the potential born of complex mental development, unsurpassed in the animal kingdom. It enables man to manipulate the environment to suit his own desires and comforts. Scientists are concerned with the origin and development of man's culture. In this connection it is to be remembered that the oldest fragments of written human history go back only to 5000 years while the Prehistoric human record is two million years old. Man (like Australopithecus/Homo erectus) used stone tools principally large hand-axes made from pebbles. These tools show a progressive advance in design and workman ship through middle Pleistocene times. Like Australopithecus, Homo erectus used stone tools principally large hand-axes made from pebbles. These tools show a progressive advance in design and workman ship through middle Pleistocene times.

Most specimens of Homo erectus have been found in sediments that range in age from about 700,000 to 200,000 years. Fossil men of our own species first occur about 500,000 years ago and were therefore contemporaneous with Homo erectus for about 200,000 years. With Australopithecus and Homo erectus fossil specimens of Homo sapiens have commonly been described as other species. The best known example is "Neanderthal man", a large boned race that lived about 100,000 years ago. But throughout the Pleistocene period fossil skulls, bones and teeth of men are rare in comparison with his stone tools.

Anthropologists recognized three principal stages in man's cultural evolutions :

(1) Palaeolithic or Old Stone Age with sub divisions of lower middle and upper characterized by chipped stone tools.

(2) Neolithic or New Stone Age characterized by ground and polished stone tools.

(3) The age of metals when tools were made first of Copper and Bronze and later of Iron.

Palaeolithic or Old Stone Age : Palaeolithic tools show a progressive improvement in tool making techniques—the Block-on-Block, the Stone Hammer, the Cylindrical Stone Hammer, Levellois, Mousterian and others. The earliest are crude hand axes and the most advance are the carefully styled projectile points and knives made by Late Palaeolithic men. The Late Palaeolithic men used bone for making fine tools such as needles. In his long prehistoric history, man in the beginning had to depend on hunting and gathering of wild plants. Thus he was a food gatherer. But in the Late Pleistocene period he started domesticating animals and growing his own food.

Chapter —II

Geological and Anthropological Background

Plate Ia

Kinds of Rocks and Techniques in Making Stone Tools

1. Block-on-Block Technique or Anvil Technique
2. Stone Hammer Technique
   a) Application of Stone Hammer Over Proposed Tool
   b) Faces (Front and Back) of the Flake Removed
3. Cylindrical Hammer Technique
4. Levalloisian Technique
   a, b, c, d). Application of Levalloisian Technique
5. Mousterian Technique
6. Pressure Technique

Plate Ib

Ancestor of Modern Humans (Chipped Stones like Hatchets, Axes and Knives)

Plate II

Of the 193 species of monkeys and apes, 192 are covered with hair except the naked ape. The naked ape is a primate like Chimpanzee, Gorilla and Gibbon but with some difference. All these were forest creatures. About 15 million years ago this forest strong holds were reduced in size and the naked ape left the forest. In the last million years vital changes took place.

Our ancestors became more upright; their hands freed from locomotion and were efficient to hold weapons. They were physically well equipped. The hunting ape was in the making. Brain growth prolonged to adult size. He began using artificial weapons instead of natural ones since he was less fit for obtaining food than the other carnivores. He became a co-operative pack hunter to survive, which led to home base.

Plate III

Solar System and the Structure of Earth

Scientists believe 100 billion years ago in the open space, the earth on which we live, the sun and all other planets of solar system were in the form of cloud of cold dust particles swirling through empty space. Gradually these particles were attracted together in the form of a spinning disk. As it spun disk separated in the rings in the furious motion and made the particles white-hot. Thus the solar system was formed. The effect of sun, on earth and other planets result in the form of day and night, climate fluctuations, seasons and others.

The earth is like a giant baseball. The solid rock covering the surface is 600 miles deep and is called crust. The rocky portion below it is 1800 miles and it is called mantle. Below the mantle, at the centre is the core in the form of hot liquid and solid-magma.

Plate IV

Geological Record

Earth is like a giant Baseball or Rosette stone. Locked with in the layers of rock beneath our feet, lie the secrets of earth creation and characteristics of time. It is in the form of sedimentary deposits and fossilized remains of creatures. In the beginning there was no life on earth. Afterwards this lifeless nature prepared for the first microscopic living organism. These organisms were destroyed and extinct. After that through endless subtle mutations, they evolved into new forms of life. These broad gaps over a billion years in the slow development of life are broadly divided as the Paleozoic (Ancient) era, Mesozoic (Middle) era and Cenozoic (Recent) era.

In the succeeding layers geologists and anthropologists find other clues to the mystery of time and life: the appearance of the lowest forms of animal life such as worms, jelly fish about five million years ago; the evolution of fish, reptiles, birds and mammals, including primitive man. Late in this order traces of strange and wonderful animals appear. About only one million years ago man first appeared on the geological record.

Plate V

Physical Evolution of Man

Oldest fragments of written human history go back to 5000 years. But the Prehistoric human record is two million years old. The origin of man and the history of primate ancestors has been understood from the fossils discovered.

Man's closest relatives—the "Pre-Monkeys, Monkeys and Apes"—that along with man and his extinct ancestors make up the mammalian order of primates. The grasping hands and stereoscopic vision arose in primates as adoptions for life in trees. These two features are the foundation of man's later evolutionary success on the ground for they permitted him to grasp tools and weapons and to co-ordinate hand and vision precisely.

The primate stage gave rise to second order, the anthropoid monkey, apes and men. Fossils of a group of generalized apes called "Dryopithecines" these are ancestral both to man and Chimpanzee, Gorilla and Orangutan. Man's most characteristic feature in which he differs from all other relatives is his extraordinary large brain:

The fossil record of the Pleistocene period revealed that there are only three main stages in the man's physical evolution, (1) Australopith in the early Pleistocene, (2) Homo erectus in the middle Pleistocene and (3) Homo sapien in the late Pleistocene.

Australopithecus (other types Ramapithecus and Homo): The brain volume was 600-700cu.cm i.e., half of modern brain. His upright stance freed the hands from the use in locomotion, instead they could now be used exclusively for tool making and weapon throwing.

Homo erectus : The fossils are found in Java, China, Africa, Asia and Europe. His brain volume is intermediary between Australopithecus and modern man. He used stone tools such as large hand axes. Best known example is Neanderthal.

Homo sapien : His fossil record is rare in comparison to stone tools.

Evidence found by scientists in the mountains of Iraq (Shandal) reveal that man has been living on earth for one million years.

REFERENCES

Felix Sutton	1960	Our earth Printed in the United States of America.
Stokes, W. L.	1965	*Essentials of Earth History*, Pentice - Hall Of India (Private Ltd.) New Delhi.
Butzer, K. W.	1964	*Environment and Archaeology*, Metheun And Company Ltd., London.
A. Lee Mc. Alester,	1969	*The History of Life*, Pentice - hall of India (Private Ltd.) New Delhi.
Khan, E.	1968	*Pleistocene Strategy in India*, Annals of Geological Volume, Aligarh.
Thakur, S. C.	1987	*Evolution : The Missing Link*, Science Express September 1, 1987.

Chapter—III

Lower Palaeolithic Period (500,000–55,000 B. P.)

In India discoveries of the Palaeolithic and Post Palaeolithic evidences are made from the last part of the 19th century. But the finds are sporadic and isolated in nature. Geologists like Oldham (1864), King (1872), Foote (1884), Civil Servicemen like Sewell (1882), Moir (1909), and Brackenbury (1940), Commaid (1930) and missionaries like Manley (1935) are credited with such discoveries. From the stage of simple discoveries Commaide and Burkit studied different stages and techniques in making tools. Subsequently Soundara Rajan made an attempt towards the understanding of the Palaeolithic in stratified context and chronological order in his discoveries at Nagarjunakonda and Giddalur. Another important development is the artifacts of the Prehistoric Period are studied in the context of environment, economy, society etc., Sankalia (1974), Mishra and Bellwood (1985), Sankalia and his associates G. R. Sarma, B. Subbarao, state and central government departments of Archaeology conducted intensive explorations. Now the Prehistorians are concerned as much with spacio-temporal aspects of Stratigraphical and tech-temporal aspects as with the interdisciplinary research for having insights into life ways of the prehistoric people.

In Andhra Pradesh since the discovery of Prehistoric tools by Robert Bruce Foote in 1916, a number of scholars have been undertaking Prehistoric researches in the inland areas, river systems and the areas of sea levels. Burkitt and Commaide (1930) gave a frame to Prehistory of Andhra Pradesh on the tool technology by arranging them in four stages - Series I, II, III, and IV. Later Soundara Rajan (1952-58) attempted to establish stratigraphical context of the Palaeolithic tools at Giddalur and Nagarjunakonda. Subsequently studies were carried out by number of scholars: Isaac (1960) in Kurnool, Murthy (1966) in Chittor, S. N. Rao (1966) in Nalgonda, Timma Reddy (1968) in Cuddapah, Sudarshan (1979) in Nellore, Madhusoodana Rao (1979) in Prakasham District, Krishna Sastry (1980) in Amarabad Valley in Nallamalai ranges in Mahaboobnagar district, Prakash (1981) in Ghambhiram Valley of Vijag district, Kasturi (1980) Yeleswaram river valley of Godavari, Bhaskara Murthy (1980-1981) Seetapally and other valleys of the Godavari Basin, B.R. Subrahmanyam and D.L.N. Sastry (1980-85) Manjra valley in Medak district and the sea levels in Nellore and Prakasam Districts.

In India artifacts of the Palaeolithic period are found in the middle Pleistocene deposits in the peninsular and extra peninsular areas.

Artifacts of the Lower Palaeolithic period are found in the middle Pleistocene period in the peninsular area where the remains of two wet and dry phases are evidenced by the deposition of gravel and silt. In the lower gravel (gravel I) remains of the Lower Palaeolithic period are found. In the extra peninsular area the artifacts are found associated with the earliest two terraces.

It is generally felt that there existed two different cultural groups, the "Soan" and the Madrasian. The "Soan" cultural group in the extra peninsular area is characterized by chopper, chopping tools and massive crude flakes from pebble. The other group the "Madrasian" belongs to peninsula, comprised of bi-facially worked implements of Acheulian tradition - hand-axes and cleavers. (Krishna Swamy 1948).

In the subsequent analysis typo-technological variations are also noticed. In identifying lower, middle and upper Palaeolithic sites, artifact concentration is generally taken as criteria. The sites found in plateau, pene-plain or plains are generally located in the context of some kind of drainage system. Generally, artifacts of the Lower, Middle and Upper Palaeolithic Periods are found in a mixed condition and rarely in an exclusive state.

Plate VI

Lower Palaeolithic Period : Choppers, Chopping Tools, Heavy Duty Tools and other Hand-Axe Types Abbevillian and Acheulian types of the Lower Palaeolithic Period collected on the left bank of Krishna at Yeleswaram, Andhra Pradesh.

1, 2, 3. **Choppers on Pebbles**
4, 5..7. **Chopping Tools and Pebbles**
8, 10,...19. **Hand-Axe Types**

Description of Tools

1. (YLM) Chopper on a thick flat based elongated oval pebble of Grey Quartzite, working edge is obtained by the removal of deep and shallow flakes from the flat surface upwards, fresh. (138×103×66mm)

2. (MDR) Chopper on the flat based oval pebble of Brown Quartzite, convex cutting edge is produced by the removal of three shallow flakes from the flat surface upwards, fresh. (83×104×33mm)

3. (CGP) Chopper on a roughly flat based, circular pebble of Grey Quartzite, convex cutting edge is produced by the removal of shallow flakes from the flat surface upwards, fresh. (5×77×41mm)

4. (YLM) Chopping tool (bi-facial chopper) on a thick roundish pebble of Brown Quartzite, convex working edge is obtained by the intersection of deep and shallow flake scars from two faces, fresh. (77×81×58mm)

5. (NGM) Chopping tool on a thick elongated oval pebble of Brown Quartzite, convex working edge is obtained by the removal of shallow and deep flakes from either surfaces, fresh. (100×68×58mm)

6. (KDK) Chopping tool on a small flat based circular pebble of Brown Quartzite, broad convex working edge is produced by the removal of shallow flakes from either faces, fresh. (64×85×39mm)

7. (KDK) Chopping tool on a thick flat based rounded pebble of Brown Quartzite, convex working edge is obtained by the intersection of deep and shallow flake scars from two faces, fresh. (108×109×68mm)

8. (YLM) Elongated pear-shaped crude and heavy hand axe on a pebble, Brown Quartzite. Fully flaked on one surface leaving a small patch of cortex at the butt end, unworked with a mid ridge on the other surface except for the removal of a shallow flake at the working end and a deep flake at the butt end, slightly broken at the tip. Line of profile is slightly wavy. Asymmetrical, biconvex cross-section, fresh. (215×120×98mm)

9. (VGR) Elongated oval crude and heavy hand axe on a chunk of Dolerite, flaked on both surfaces showing shallow and deep large flake scars. Broken at the tip. Line of profile slightly wavy, fresh. (210×145×88mm)

10. (AMB) Triangular-shaped crude and heavy hand axe on a pebble of brown Cherty Quartzite, flaked on either surfaces, showing shallow and deep flake scars, line of profiles slightly wavy, thick in the centre by conical cross section at the centre, fresh (200×130×106mm).

11. (YLM) Crude and heavy hand axe made on irregular triangular shaped chunk of Grey Quartzite working end is neatly prepared and tongue shaped butt end is bifacially worked but less worked and is very thick, line of profile slightly wavy, fresh (182×144×104mm).

12. (VGR) Elongated pear shaped hand axe on a chunk of Dolerite bi-facially worked showing large and small and deep shallow flake scars. Pointed tip is slightly broken, line of profile slightly wavy, biconvex cross-section, fresh. (223×122×95mm)

13. (VGR) Oval shaped crude hand axe made on a chunk of Brown Quartzite, bifacially worked with shallow and deep flake scars and also large and small in nature, line of profile slightly wavy, cross-section Asymmetrical, biconvex, irregular, fresh. (144×110×52mm)

14. (YLM) Elongated oval shaped hand axe on a thick side-flake of Brown Quartzite. Upper surface shows large deep and shallow flake scars leaving a patch of original surface towards butt end on the left margin. Under surface is flaked all along the margins leaving a part of primary flake surface in the centre, working end is pointed brown, wavy cross section, Asymmetrical fresh (178×110×60mm).

15. (AMBD) Oval shaped hand axe on a chunk of dark Brown Quartzite. Both surfaces flaked and shows deep and shallow large flake scars, thick towards the butt end, comparatively thin and pointed, towards the working end. The specimen is under preparation, line of profile wavy, cross section irregular plano-convex, fresh. (148×97×66mm)

16. (DPD) Pear shaped medium sized hand axe on a chunk of Grey Quartzite. Both faces fully flaked and characterized by numerous shallow and deep flake scars, thick at the centre. Tip is thin and slightly broken. Line of profile wavy. Cross -section Asymmetrical, fresh. (179×97×75mm)

17. Almond-shaped a small crude hand axe on a chunk of Brown Quartzite. Bifacially flaked with shallow and deep flake scars, thick at the centre. The tip is pointed and slightly broken. Butt end is rounded. Line of profile is slightly wavy, cross - section biconical, fresh. (106×80×52mm)

18. (INL) Elongated pear-shaped small pebble. Hand axe on a pale Grey Quartzite. Both faces flaked leaving a patch of cortex on both the faces near the butt. Tip pointed, central ridge on both the surfaces. Butt end thick. Lines of profile is slightly wavy, cross section plano convex, fresh (134×63×49mm).

19. (YLM) Elongated oval-shaped small hand axe made on a chunk of Grey Quartzite, Bifacially worked. Flake scars mainly shallow and occasionally deep on both faces, Tip rounded and slightly broken. Thick at the centre, Line of profile slightly wavy, biconvex cross section slightly effaced. (110×68×54mm)

Plate VII

Hand-axes, Miniature Hand-axes showing working on both the faces of the Lower Palaeolithic period found in different parts of Andhra Pradesh.

1, 2...13	**Hand-axe types**
14, 15, 16	**Miniature Hand-axes on Flakes**

DESCRIPTION OF TOOLS

1. (VGR) Triangular-shaped hand axe on a pebble of pale grey fine grained Quartzite. Bifacially worked with small shallow flake scars, symmetrical outline, comparatively thick at the centre. Lateral margins are converging into a point at the working end. Tip

is slightly broken. Butt end is broad and comparatively thicker than the tip. Line of profile slightly wavy. Cross-section biconvex, fresh. (122×96×42mm)

2. (RSPM) Elongated oval shaped hand axe on a thin chunk of pale Brown Quartzite. Both faces fully flaked and characterized by numerous small and shallow flake scars. Symmetrical outline, comparatively thicker at the centre, tip slightly broken, butt end comparatively thicker than the tip. Line of profile is almost straight, cross section biconvex, fresh. (165×105×40mm)

3. (VGR) Pear shaped hand axe on a pebble of Quartzite. Bifacially worked leaving a patch of cortex at the butt end. Both faces show small shallow flake scars. Tip is slightly broken and is tongue shaped. Butt end is thick, comparatively less worked and shows a deep small flake scar on one of the faces. Line of profile slightly wavy, cross-section biconvex, fresh.

4. (IRP) Pear-shaped hand-axe on a chunk of Quartzite, bi-facially worked and characterized by deep and shallow flake scars and also large and small lateral margins trimmed and shows minute flake scars. The tip is thin and tongue shaped, thick at the centre and also at the butt end, line of profile slightly wavy, cross-section bi-convex, fresh. (143×85×40mm)

5. (CRL) Pear-shaped hand-axe on a chunk of dark Brown Quartzite, bi-facially worked with small shallow and deep flake scars. Trimmed at the lateral margins, intentional groove is made on the upper surface perhaps to facilitate hafting, thick at the centre. Butt end is less worked, tip is comparatively thin and tongue shaped, line of profile slightly wavy, cross-section bi-convex, fresh. (156×85×50mm)

6. (VGR) Oval shaped hand-axe on a chunk of dark Brown Quartzite, upper surface fully worked and characterized by deep and shallow numerous flake scars, under surface comparatively less worked leaving a patch of primary flake surface towards butt. The flake scars are characterized by both deep and large, as well as small and shallow. Working end is pointed and butt end is broad and rounded. Thick at the centre, symmetrical out line and line of profile is slightly wavy, cross-section is biconvex, fresh.

7. (KPM) Pear shaped hand-axe on a chunk of Brown Quartzite, bifacially flaked with shallow and deep, large and small flake scars. Thick at the centre, and tongue shaped at the working end. Butt end is comparatively thick, minutely worked along the periphery. Line of profile slightly wavy, cross-section bi-convex, and fresh. (151×93×44 mm)

8. (VGR) Rostrocarinate type small hand-axe on coarse grained Quartzite. Bi-facially worked, one of the surface shows shallow and small flake scars and the other surface shows numerous small flake scars, thick at the centre, broad and thick butt end,

comparatively thin and narrow beak like working end. Line of profile wavy, cross-section bi-convex, fresh.

9. (VGR) Round elongated oval shaped hand-axe on brown coarse grained Quartzite, bi-facially flaked, one of the surfaces shows small, shallow and deep flake scars. The other surface shows large, deep flake scars forming a ridge from the centre to the tip and small shallow flake scars towards butt end. Thick at the centre lateral margin trimmed and converging into a pointed working end slightly broken, butt end broad and rounded, symmetrical outline, line of profile slightly wavy, cross-section bi-convex, fresh. (110×85×43mm)

10. (IML) Elongated oval hand-axe on chunk of Brown Quartzite, fully flaked on either faces, by step flaking. One of the faces shows deep and shallow numerous flake scars, the other face shows too large and shallow, numerous small flake scars, working end is thin and tongue shaped, butt end thick, line of profile slightly wavy, cross-section lenticular, fresh. (139×89×36mm)

11. (MRP) Elongated oval shaped hand-axe made on a side flake of fine grained Grey Quartzite. Bi-facially worked one of the surfaces show shallow large and small flake scars. The other surface shows a large flake scar towards the working end and a very small shallow flake scars towards the butt end. The specimen is neatly trimmed all along the periphery. Working end is thin and of spatula shape with neat workman ship. Butt end is comparatively thick and broad. Line of profile is straight, fresh. (120×83×36 mm)

12. (NDP) Oval shaped hand-axe made on a flake of Brown Quartzite. Upper surface shows small, shallow flake scars. Under surface shows a small shallow flake scar all along the periphery leaving a patch of primary flake surface at the centre. Working end is comparatively narrow and thin. Butt end is round and symmetrical in out line. Line of profile is slightly wavy. Cross-section is plano-convex. Fresh.

13. (KMK) Leaf shaped small hand-axe on a pale Grey fine grind Quartzite. Fully worked with numerous shallow flake scars on either face. Symmetrical in outline. Working end pointed with a small ridge at the centre on either surface. Butt end is comparatively broad than the working end. Neat workmanship all along the periphery. Line of profile is slightly wavy. Bi-convex cross-section, fresh. (125×61×27mm)

14. (INL) Elongated oval-shaped hand-axe made on a broad and large thick side flake of Quartzite, bi-facially worked by step flaking. Upper surface shows two deep and two shallow flake scars in the centre surrounded by numerous very small shallow flake scars all along the periphery. Under surface shows a large shallow flake scar in the centre surrounded by numerous shallow and deep flake scars. Symmetrical in out line and the periphery shows trimming. Butt end is comparatively broad and the tip is

comparatively narrow with working edge all along the periphery, line of profile is slightly wavy, cross-section plano-convex, fresh. (178×112×30mm)

15. (MCP) Miniature hand-axe of elongated oval shape made on a thick end flake of Brown Quartzite. Thick in the centre, slightly pointed on either end bifacially worked showing numerous small shallow and few deep flake scars. Neatly trimmed all along the periphery; line of profile slightly wavy cross-section biconvex, fresh. (102×56×27mm)

16. (INL) Oval shaped small thin hand-axe on a chunk of Brown Quartzite. Bifacially worked with small shallow flake scars. Tip is slightly pointed and but end broad and round. Neatly trimmed all along the periphery. Sharp cross section, and is slightly wavy, biconvex, fresh.

17. (MCP) Triangular-shaped small hand-axe made on thin end flake of dark Brown Quartzite, bifacially worked numerous small shallow flake scars are predominant lateral margins are converging in to a point at the tip. The broad rounded butt end is made as a small tang by removing two deep flake scars on either margins to facilitate hafting, the two lateral margins show excellent workmanship on either face to form a sharp cutting edges, symmetrical out line, line of profile is roughly wavy, fresh. (113×83×25mm)

18. (MCP) Heart shaped small hand-axe on thin brown end flake of Quartzite, fully worked on either faces by step flaking and shows numerous small shallow flake scars, symmetrical in out line, line of profile slightly wavy the entire margin is trimmed and shows sharp cutting edge. The tip is slightly pointed and the butt end is broad and rounded, cross-section lenticular, fresh. (97×85×28mm)

Plate VIII

Cleaver types with different butts (holding portions)

1, 2, 8.	**Cleaver with 'U'-shaped butt and convex cutting edge**
3, 5, 12.	**Cleaver with 'U'-shaped butt and straight cutting edge**
7, 14, 17.	**Cleaver with 'U'-shaped butt and obliquc cutting edge**
16.	**'U'-shaped cleaver with straight cutting edge (hafted)**
4, 11, 15.	**Cleaver with 'V'-shaped butt and oblique cutting edge**
6.	**Cleaver with 'V'-shaped butt and straight cutting edge**
9.	**Cleaver with 'V'-shaped butt and concave cutting edge**
10.	**Cleaver with 'V'-shaped butt and convex cutting edge**

DESCRIPTION OF CLEAVER TYPES

1. (YLM) 'U' shaped crude and heavy cleaver with rectangular butt end, cleaver

edge is convex, upper surface fully worked except a small portion on left lateral margin, under surface unworked except at the working end and one of the lateral margins, cross-section roughly rectangular, fresh. (175×108×65mm)

2. (AMR) 'U' shaped crude and heavy cleaver on a thick flake of Brown Quartzite. Upper surface fully flaked with large and small flake scars of shallow and deep in nature. Thick at the centre on the upper surface, under surface shows large deep flake scars with a patch of primary flake surface, upper surface thick at the centre, cutting edge convex, lateral sides fully trimmed, cross-section plano-convex, fresh. (152×102×70mm)

3. (YCM) 'U' shaped crude cleaver on thick flake of Grey Quartzite lateral sides straight and converge towards butt cutting edge straight, upper surface partly flaked towards cutting edge under surface flaked along the lateral margins, cross-section plano-convex, Fresh.154×122×58mm.

4. 'V' shaped crude cleaver on a chunk of Brown Quartzite. Upper surface is fully flaked with deep and shallow flake scars, of large & small nature. Undersurface is flaked along the two lateral margins and also at the butt end, leaving a patch of primary flake surface from centre to the cutting edge. Cleaver edge is oblique, cross-section asymmetrical bi-convex, fresh. (172×100×53mm)

5. (CRL) 'U' shaped crude cleaver on a thick flake of a pebble of Brown Quartzite. Upper surface is thick at the centre and partly flaked leaving a patch of cortex on the left side half of the tool. Under surface is flaked only along the lateral margin and at the butt end, cleaver edge is straight, cross-section plano-convex, fresh. (141×95×50mm)

6. 'V' shaped cleaver on thick side flake of a pebble of Brown Quartzite. Upper surface flaked only along the left lateral margin and consists of a large deep and a few small shallow, flake scars. The remaining surface is unworked and covered by pebble cortex. Under surface is also partly flaked. Trimmed along the broad working edge, the lateral margin cleaver edge is roughly straight, cross-section asymmetrical bi-convex, fresh. (160×123×46mm)

7. (CRL) 'U' shaped cleaver on a thick side flake of Brown Quartzite. Upper surface is fully flaked except in the centre and near the working edge. Undersurface is flaked along lateral margins. Cutting edge extending from the centre and towards but end, leaving a large patch of primary flake surface. Thick at the centre cleaver edge is straight and shows use-marks. Cross-section asymmetrical bi-convex, fresh. (153×95×53 mm)

8. (AMBD) Irregular 'U' shaped cleaver on a thick side flake of Brown Quartzite. Cleaver edge convex and trimmed from under surface, thick in the centre. Butt end is slightly projected and slightly made thin bi- facial flaking. Upper surface is fully flaked

and shows a few, large and shallow flake scars on the right half, numerous small and comparatively deep flake scars by step cutting on the left half of the specimen. Under surface flaked along the left lateral margin, partly which continued on the butt end leaving a large portion of main flake surface, cross-section asymmetrical bi-convex, fresh. (163×103×44mm)

9. (YLM) 'V' shaped cleaver on a flake of Brown Quartzite. Cleaver edge is concave. Both surfaces fully worked. Flake scars are large and small & deep and shallow in nature. Lateral sides fully trimmed fresh. (154×100×45mm)

10. (AMBD) 'V' shaped cleaver on a thin flake of Brown Quartzite Cleaver edge is convex. One of the surfaces show a central large and shallow flake scar extending to the butt end; the other surface shows, step flaking along the lateral sides leaving a large primary flake surface. The margins are fully trimmed near the platform, fresh. (138×110×35mm)

11. 'V' shaped cleaver on a flake of dark Brown Quartzite. Cleaver edge is oblique.

Upper surface is fully flaked and shows two, deep and large flake scars at the centre and shallow and small flake scars along the sides. The lower surface is partially worked with primary flake surface, fresh. (157×90×38mm)

12. (CRL) 'U' shaped cleaver on a thick Brown Quartzite. Cleaver edge is straight. Upper surface partially flaked with large and deep flake scars and also small and shallow flake scars. Lower surface is unworked except at the left lateral margin, fresh. (142×99×49mm)

13. (AMBD) 'V' shaped cleaver on a flake of Brown Quartzite. Clearer edge is in convex shape. Upper surface partially worked with small shallow flake scars. Undersurface shows bulb of percussion and main flake surface. The right later margin is steeply flaked from the under surface, while the left lateral margin is worked from the upper surface, fresh. (118×81×35mm)

14. 'U' shaped cleaver on one end flake of Brown Quartzite. Cleaver edge oblique in nature with a small oblique notch. Upper surface fully flaked with small shallow flake scars and with thin brown red patination. Under surface is flaked on the bulbar portion and along the later margins, leaving a small patch of primary flake surface at the centre. Fully trimmed all along the periphery, fresh. (104×68×27mm)

15. (AMBD) 'V' shaped cleaver on a medium sized brown banded Quartzite. Cleaver edge is oblique. Upper surface is fully flaked with a large centered flake scar surrounded by small shallow flake scars on all the three sides. Under surface is worked with a prominent bulb of percussion and the main flake surfaces trimmed along the periphery, fresh. (128×98×36mm)

16. (DMV) 'U' shaped cleaver on a medium sided flake of Brownish Quartzite. Upper surface is fully flaked with small shallow flake scars. Under surface is fully flaked with a large central flake scar to obtain cleaver edge extending from the butt end surrounded by small shallow flake scars on the lateral margins. Fully trimmed along the lateral margins, creating a wavy edge probably to facilitate hafting, fresh. (107×60×27 mm)

17. (MRP) 'U' shaped medium sized, cleaver on a side-flake. Cleaver edge is oblique and thick near the surface portion. Upper surface fully flaked with a large shallow flake-scar extending from butt end to working end, surrounded by small shallow flake scars flaked from the under surface. Under surface is partially flaked especially on the left haft of the tool steeply flaked from the under surface, fully trimmed all along the periphery, fresh. (103×58×39mm)

Plate IX

General Tool Types Arranged in Order of Evolution

1. Pebble 6. Spatula 18. Borer 26. Minia-ture Hand-Axe	2. Chopper 7,8. Knives 19. Core 27. Fabricator-Cum-Borer	3. Chopping Tool 11. Cleaver 20. Fabricator	4. Bi-facial tool 12,13. Chisels 21,25. Hand-axes Cum-Borer	5,9,10. Discoid 14,15,..17 Spheroids 22,23,24 Picks

DESCRIPTION OF TOOL TYPES

1. (MCP) Pebble of dark Brown Quartzite in Spheroid shape. Rolled.

2. Chopper on a flat pebble. A chip is removed and left untouched. The flake portion is patinated.

3. Uni-facial chopper on a dark Brown Quartzite with deep and shallow flake scars on the ventral side.

4. Bi-facial chopper on a Brown Quartzite cutting edge is obtained by removing deep and shallow flake scars by alternate flaking.

5. (YLM) Discoid made on thick end flake of dark Brown Quartzite. Upper surface fully flaked with large and deep, small and shallow flake scars. Under surface is partly flaked with a bulb of percussion and flake surface is primary. Working edges slightly wavy and runs all around the periphery. Fresh.

6. A miniature spatula on end flake of Brown Quartzite bi-facially and fully worked. Minutely numerous small and shallow flake scars are predominant. Thick at the centre from the upper surface, working edge is thin, sharp and tongue shaped. Butt end is thick, and convex, it is carefully trimmed all around the periphery. Line of profile is almost straight, triangular cross-section, fresh.

7. (YLM) Knife on a residual core of Quartzite. It's edge is prepared on the convex side by removal of minute flakes from the under surface. Both the faces show large and small, shallow and deep flake scars. Fresh.

8. (KMK) A knife with beak shaped projection on a rectangular flake of Brown Quartzite, working is visible all along the periphery. Both the faces are flaked forming irregular ridges on either of the surface. Slight notch is visible on the right lateral margin towards the tip, which gives a beak like projection to the tool. Line of profile slightly wavy and thick. Lime encrustation is present on the upper surface. Fresh.

9. (YLM) Discoid made on thick end flake of dark Brown Quartzite. Upper surface fully flaked with large and deep, small and shallow flake scars. Under surface is partly flaked with a bulb of percussion and flake surface is primary. Working edges slightly wavy and runs all around the periphery. Fresh.

10. (YLN) Discoid made on thick end flake of dark Brown Quartzite. Upper surface fully worked. Shallow flake scars are prominent and numerous. Under surface mostly worked, leaving a patch of primary flake surface with small, deep and shallow flake scars. Working edge almost straight and runs all around the periphery. Fresh.

11. (INL) Cleaver on a rectangular shaped thin chunk of Quartzite. Upper surface shows large, deep and shallow flake scars removed from the under surface. Under surface is flat at the centre and tapers to the periphery by means of step flaking. The entire periphery is trimmed from both sides to obtain a sharp cutting edge. A multipurpose tool for cutting, chopping, skimming etc.

12. (AMBD) A shaped chisel on a chunk of dark Brown Quartzite. Upper surface shows large and small, deep and shallow flake scars converging into a ridge at the centre. Under surface shows large and deep, small and shallow flake scars with a longitudinal ridge. Butt end is thick and blunted with numerous small flake scars to facilitate hand-hold. Working end is thin and almost straight. Fresh.

13. (AMBD) Double-edged chisel made on rectangular thin chunk of dark Brown Quartzite. Both surfaces are fully worked by alternate flaking from the lateral margins for facilitating hand-hold. Working edges are obtained on either end by removal of minute flakes from either face, fresh.

14. (VGR) Spheroid on core of Grey Quartzite with a thin brownish red occasional

patina. Both faces fully worked. Flake scars are of both large and small, shallow and deep nature. Working edge almost straight and runs all around the periphery. Fresh.

15. Spheroid made on a thin core of Brown Quartzite. Both faces fully worked. Flake scars both large, small and also shallow in nature. Working edge is slightly wavy and runs all around the periphery. Fresh.

16. Spheroid made on thin flat pebble of Brown Quartzite. Upper surface partly flaked retaining pebble cortex on ¾th of the specimen. Under surface is fully flaked leaving a small portion of pebble cortex. Flake scars are both large and small and shallow in nature, working edge is almost straight and runs all around the periphery. Fresh.

17. (MKD) Spheroid on a thin flat core of pinkish Quartzite. Both surfaces fully flaked; shallow small flake scars are predominant. Working edge is almost straight and runs all around the periphery. Fresh.

18. Borer on a thick irregular shaped and flake of Brown Quartzite. Upper surface fully flaked with large and small shallow flake scars. Under surface shows main flake surface with a bulb of percussion. Scraping edge is prepared opposite to the bulbar end by minute flaking on the margin, from under surface. Borer point is obtained on the left lateral margin. Fresh.

19. (YLM) Core scraper on a chunk of dark Brown Quartzite. Deep and shallow flake scars towards the sides and flat at the centre, surround both the surfaces. Scraping edge is restricted to the part of the periphery worked from the under surface. Fresh.

20. Fabricator.

21. (VGR) Hand-axe with a beak shaped projection on a roughly triangular thin chunk of Brown Quartzite. Bifacially worked. Flake scars are large and small and deep and shallow in nature forming irregular ridges on either surfaces. Working edge is thin and sharp meant for cutting grass, need the fibers. It may be a prototype penknife meant for cutting the fibers. Line of profile is slightly wavy. Asymmetric. Cross-section is biconvex. Fresh.

22. (DPD) Elongated pear shaped pick on a pebble of Grey Quartzite. Either surface flaked and shows shallow and deep, large and small flake scars. A longitudinal ridge is on either side, thick at the centre and thin down to the working end. Butt end retains pebble cortex. Line of profile is slightly wavy. Cross-section is tetrahedral, fresh.

23. (DPD) Pear shaped medium sized hand axe (pick) on a pebble of Brown Quartzite. Upper surface partly flaked with shallow flake scars forming an incipient median ridge extending from centre to the tip leaving pebble cortex towards the butt end. Under surface fully flaked with large and small shallow flake scars trimmed along

the two lateral margins. Tip pointed, the line of profile is slightly wavy, cross-section plano-convex, fresh.

24. (MEP) Pear shaped medium sized pick on a pebble of Brown Quartzite. Thin bright brownish patina all over the body. Butt is thick and rounded with pebble cortex. Tip is narrow thin and pointed. Both the surfaces with a mid ridge show large, shallow and deep flake scars extending from the centre. Line of profile slightly wavy. Cross section asymmetric biconvex.

25. Hand axe.

26. (DPD) Roughly triangular shaped hand-axe on medium sized chunk of gray Quartzite. Both surfaces fully flaked with a slight ridge on either side flake scars both large and small and shallow and deep in nature. Line of profile is slightly wavy tip narrow, and tongue shaped. Butt is thick and broad with lime encrustation. Cross-section is quadrangular. Fresh.

27. (KDK) Elongated triangular shaped fabricator cum borer on a chunk of Brown Quartzite. Upper surface is steeply flaked all along the lateral margins leaving the original surface. Under surface is fully flaked with small shallow and deep flake scars. Tip converging into pointed end. Butt end is thick. Line of profile is slightly wavy. Cross-sections a roughly triangular, fresh.

28. (DPD) Elongated roughly triangular shaped medium sized pick on a primary flake of Brown Quartzite. Upper surface is steeply flaked. Under surface is fully flaked with shallow and deep, large and small flake scars. Tip is narrow and pointed. Butt end is broad. Line of profile slightly wavy. Cross-section is trapezoidal. Fresh.

Plate X

Type-sites: Yeleswaram and Amarabad in the valley of river Krishna
Tool assemblage-showing economy

'L' BOARD	'A' BOARD	'P' BOARD
1. Pear shaped hand axe on a pebble of Brown Quartzite 2. Elongated pear shaped hand axe on a pebble of Brown Quartzite 3. Cardate shaped hand axe on a pebble of Brown Quartzite 4. Pear shaped hand axe on Brown Quartz pebble 5. 'V' shaped cleaver with a straight cutting edge. 6. 'U' shaped cleaver with a concave cutting edge of Brown Quartzite 7. 'U' shaped cleaver with a convex cutting edge of Brown Quartzite 8. Chisel with double cutting edges on a pebble of Brown Quartzite. 9. Chunk of Brown Quartzite 10. Perforator on a triangular flake.	1. (DPD) Miniature hand axe on Quartzite 2. (MCP) Miniature hand axe on Quartzite 3. (IRP) Miniature hand axe on Quartzite 4. (IRP) Miniature hand axe on Quartzite 5. Miniature pick on Quartz 6. Miniature pick on Quartz 7. (MCP) Miniature pick on Quartz 8. (MCP) Miniature hand axe on pear shaped Quartz 9. (ML) Miniature hand axe on pear shaped Quartz	1. 'V' shaped cleaver with convex cutting edge on a chunk of Brown Quartzite 2. 'U' shaped cleaver with concave cutting edge on a chunk of Brown Quartzite 3. 'V' shaped cleaver with oblique cutting edge on a chunk of Brown Quartzite 4. Cleaver on a miniature pebble with convex cutting edge on Brown Quartzite. 5. Hand axe pear shaped on a pebble of Quartzite 6. Pick on a pebble of Quartzite 7. Hand axe on a chunk of dark Brown Quartzite 8. Pear shaped hand axe on a pebble of dark Brown Quartzite 9. Flake with a beak like projection on a side worked on Quartzite 10. Chopping tool made on Quartzite 11. Flake tool on Quartzite 12. Scraper on Quartzite 13. Oval shaped hand axe on a pebble of Brown Quartzite

REFERENCES

Sankalia, H. D. 1964 *Stone Age Tools Their Techniques, Names and Probable Functions,* Deccan College, Pune.

Sen, D. 1966 *The Soanian and the Pebble Tool Complex,* "Man in India", Vol.40 No.3, pp. 178-191.

Allchin, B. & R. 1968 *The Birth of Indian Civilization.*

Foote, R. B. 1916 Prehistoric and Protohistoric Antiquities Of India.

Isaac, N. 1960 *The Stone Age Cultures of Kurnool,* Ph.D., Thesis, Pune University & Deccan College libraries.

Krishna Swamy, V.D.1951 & Soundara Rajan K.V. *The Lithic Tool Industries of the Singrauli & Basin,* Ancient India No.12.

Mishra, V. N. 1962 *The Stone Age Cultures of Rajastha,* Ph.D., Thesis Deccan College Pune.

Murthy, M. L. K. 1966 *The Stone Age Cultures of Chittor,* Ph.D., Thesis Deccan College Pune.

Rao, S. N. 1966 *The Stone Age Cultures of Nalgonda,* Ph.D., Thesis Deccan College Pune.

Timma Reddy, K. 1968 *Prehistory of Cuddapah,* Ph.D., Thesis Deccan College Pune.

Soundara Rajan, K.V. 1950 *Studies in Stone Ages of Nagarjuna Konda And it's Neighbourhood* Ancient India No.14., pp. 49-113.

Paddaiah, K. 1968 *Pre and Protohistoric Investigation in Sorapoor Doab,* Ph.D. Thesis, Deccan College, Pune.

Chapter—IV

Middle Palaeolithic Period (55,000–30,000 B.P.)

Tools of the middle Palaeolithic period are found in Gravel II in the peninsular area and late "Soan" beds belonging to the extra peninsular area. The habitation locals of this phase are found in every part of the Peninsular and extra peninsular areas. But the industries of this phase constitute single cultural group known as "Nevasa" after the type-site Nevasa. Hand-axe tradition in this group is accompanied by advanced techniques of detaching flakes [Patterson and Drun Mond 1962,1993-95]. The dominant technique employed for detaching flakes is levallois followed by prepared-non-levallois technique.

Interestingly no significant variations could be noticed in the general typological groups.

Plate XI

Types of Tools Showing Change in Economy and Diversified Activity

Left Top Board (Diamond I)	**Right Top Board (Diamond III)**
1. Miniature hand axe	1. Side scraper
2. Side Scraper	2. Double side scraper
3. Double edged side scraper	3. Round scraper
4. Convex scraper	4. Asymmetric point
5. Hollow scraper	5. Hollow cum side scraper

Left Bottom Board (Diamond II)	**Right Bottom Board (Diamond IV)**
1. Flake	1. Double side scraper
2. Side cum end scraper	2. Thumb nail scraper
3. Side cum end scraper	3. Backed blade
4. Borer cum scraper	4. Borer cum scraper
5. Asymmetric point	5. Core

CENTRAL BOARD

'V'	'I'	'B'	'G'	'Y'	'O'	'R'
1. Side Scraper 2. Double Edged Side Scraper 3. Side Cum End Scraper	1. End Scraper 2. Double Edged Side Scraper	1.Side Cum Hollow Scraper 2.Notched Scraper 3.Round Scraper	1.Thumb Nail Scraper 2,3. Points	1,2,3.Borer Cum Scrapers 4.Borer Cum End Scraper	1.Oval Flake 2.Thin Flake 3.Leaf Shaped Thin Flake	1,2.Thin Rectangular Leaf Shaped Flake 3.Leaf Shaped Flake 4.Levellois Core (Centre)

DESCRIPTION OF TOOLS

DIAMOND I (LEFT TOP BOARD)

1. (VGR) Miniature hand axe on an end flake of Brown Quartzite. Butt end is broad and thick bi-facially worked. Working end is pointed and thin cross-section. (69×50×22mm)

2. (GRP) Side scraper on a rectangular end flake of dark Brown Quartzite. Upper surface shows irregular mid ridge. One of the lateral margin shows steep working along the margin from the upper surface. (87×49×21mm)

3. (TUL) Double edged side scraper on a thick rectangular end flake of dark Brown Quartzite with the tip slightly brown. Upper surface shows median ridge. Scraping edge is obtained on the lateral margins by steep working from under surface. (96×66×35mm)

4. (BDD) Convex scraper on a roughly triangular end flake of Grey Quartzite. Convex scraping edge is obtained opposite to the bulbar end from under surface. (65×10×22mm)

5. (GDA) Hollow scraper on end flake, white fine-grained quartz slightly eroded. Hollow scraping edge is obtained opposite to the bulbar end from the under surface. (70×93×19mm)

DIAMOND II (LEFT BOTTOM BOARD)

1. (AMBD) Levallois flake on a dark brown-banded Quartzite. Under surface shows bulb of percussion with prepared facetted platform. Upper surface shows a few large and small, shallow flake scars. (53×78×15mm)

2. (AMBD) Side cum end scraper on a squarish end flake of Brown Quartzite. Scraping edge is visible on one of the lateral side margins and opposite to the bulbar end by steep working from under surface. (62×69×18mm)

3. (KPM) Side cum end scraper on a thick irregular end flake of Grey fine-grained Quartzite. Upper surface shows too large and two shallow flake scars forming irregular ridges. The right lateral margin opposite to the bulbar end shows scraping edge from under surface. The left lateral margin shows a notch with secondary working. (72×90×26mm)

4. (AMBD) Borer-cum-scraper on an irregular triangular flake of dark Brown Quartzite. Upper surface shows irregular ridges with large shallow flake scars. Under surface shows diffused bulb of percussion with a main flake surface. The left lateral margin shows steep working and the working end is made pointed as a boring point. (100×56×15mm)

5. (SGK) An asymmetric point on a thick end flake of light Grey fine-grained Quartzite. Under surface shows diffused bulb of percussion with a main flake surface and facetted-striking platform. Upper surface shows many small shallow flake scars. Both the lateral margins shows secondary working tapering into point. (80×53×20mm)

DIAMOND III (RIGHT TOP BOARD)

1. (NRK) Side scraper on flake of Brown Quartzite. Upper surface is with a ridge at the top and chisel marks at the edge. (69×44×19mm)

2. (MCP) Double sided scraper on a thin flake of Brown Quartzite. Upper surface is flat without any flake scars. (66×55×13mm)

3. (MCP) Round scraper on a thin flake of Brown Quartzite. Natural flaked marks are on the upper surface. (57×43×17mm)

4. (DPD) Point asymmetric on a thin flake of dark Brown Quartzite. Ridge formed by the removal of deep flake scars on the dorsal. Retouch is made on the edges. (78×55×27mm)

5. (MCP) Hollow cum side scraper on a thick flake of Brown Quartzite. On the upper surface a ridge is formed by the removal of deep and shallow flakes. The side margin is thickened. (103×50×23mm)

DIAMOND IV (RIGHT BOTTOM BOARD)

1. (MCP) Double sided scraper on a thin flake of dark Brown Quartzite. Minute retouch is present on the edge. The upper surface has single side. (63×44×16mm)

2. (MJR) Double sided scraper on a thin flake of Cherty Quartz. The upper surface is flaked and an irregular edge is formed. Retouch is present on the edge. (52×40×15mm)

3. (MJR) Backed Blade on a thin flake of dark Brown Quartzite. The edge is with minute retouch. (71×35×17mm)

4. (MJR) Borer-cum-scraper of a blade of Chert. Margin is naturally thick while the other margin is thinned by the removal of flakes from the upper surface. Retouch is present at the point. (64×34×14mm)(MJR)

5. (MJR) Core of thick Brown Quartzite with flake scars on all sides. (72×69×45 mm)

CENTRAL BOARD

'V' 1. Side scraper on thick triangular end flake of Brown Quartzite. One of the lateral margins (left) is steeply retouched continuously on primary under surface. Upper surface shows a prominent longitudinal ridge towards right side, fresh. (90×51×21mm)

'V' 2. Double edged side scraper on triangular end flake of dark Brown Quartzite. Both the opposite lateral margins retouched on the upper surfaces to obtain straight working edge. Upper surface shows median irregular ridge thick at the centre and tapers on the edges, fresh. (101×54×23mm)

'V' 3. Side-cum-end scraper on end flake of Brown Quartzite. The left lateral margin and margin opposite to bulbar end retouched on the upper surface to form scraping edges-upper surface flaked. Under surface show main flake surface, a bulbar scar and facetted platform, fresh. (80×68×17mm)

'I' 1. End scraper on a thick triangular intermediate flake of Brown Quartzite. Margin is retouched mainly on upper surface to form convex working edge. Thick and facetted on the other two margins. Under surface is flat and tapers towards working edge, fresh. (73×58×18mm)

'I' 2. Double-edged side scraper on a rectangular flake of Brown Quartzite. Both the opposite lateral margins retouched on both the faces to obtain straight scraping edges. Upper surface is fully flaked with ridges, fresh. (122×75×27mm)

'I' 3. Double edged side scraper on thick end flake of Brown Quartzite. Both opposite lateral margins are retouched on upper surface to obtain straight working edge. Upper surface is flaked, and thick at the centre and it tapers towards the lateral margin, fresh. (80×53×26mm)

'B' 1. Side cum hollow scraper on a thick irregular flake of dark Brown Quartzite. Notch is produced by removing large flake along one of the longer lateral sides and further retouched in the notch to obtain hollow ringing edge. The opposite lateral side is retouched from both the faces to obtain straight cutting edge, fresh. (67×65×24mm)

'B' 2. Side-cum-notched scraper on an end flake of Brown Quartzite. Notch produced by removing a large flake along a part of the right longer lateral side to serve as concave scraping edge. Beyond the notch on the right lateral margin, end is retouched on the upper surface and continued further to the shorter margin, which is opposite to bulbar end. A part of the left margin is also retouched on the under surface to serve as scraping edge, fresh. (65×46×16mm)

'B' 3. Round scraper on a thick oval end flake of Brown Quartzite small flakes have been removed all along the periphery and subsequent retouch is made along the periphery on the surface to obtain convex scraping edge. Under surface shows bulbar scar and main flake surface. Upper surface shows a large and deep and many small shallow flake scars, fresh. (71×68×24mm)

'G' 1. Thumb nail scraper on a side flake of dark Brown Quartzite steeply retouched all along the periphery on both the faces. Upper surface is fully flaked and shows shallow and deep small flake scars. Under surface shows a large shallow flake scar in the centre extending the entire length and breadth of the flakes except on all the four sides, where secondary wavy working is extended, fresh. (66×41×18mm)

'G' 2. Point on thick sub-triangular end flake of Brown Quartzite; Bulb, and plain striking platform are prominent. Right lateral margin shows minute retouch on upper surface; tip pointed and shows minute retouch on one side and slight working on other sides. Upper surface shows large shallow and deep flake scars with three median ridges; fresh. (70×54×18mm)

'G' 3. Point on a triangular end flake or Brown Quartzite. Both the lateral margins show presence of tiny flake scars. Tips pointed and show minute retouch on either side, upper surface shows a median ridge with larger and smaller shallow and deep flake scars. Under surface is primary surface. In the centre, shallow large and small flake scars along the long margin.

'Y' 1. Borer cum scraper on very thick end flake of Grey Quartzite one of the lateral margins retouched, from the upper surface to obtain convex scraping edge. Other longer side is thick for handhold. Borer tip produced at the end portion of the retouched lateral side by careful working, fresh. (100×97×37mm)

'Y' 2. Borer cum scraper on a thick irregular end flake of Brown Quartzite one of the lateral margins retouched from upper surface to obtain convex scraping edge. Other longer side is thick for handhold. Borer tip produced at the end portion of the retouched lateral side by careful working, fresh. (66×54×22mm)

'Y' 3. Borer-cum-scraper on a thick irregular end flake of gray Quartzite. One of the lateral margins retouched from the upper surface to obtain convex scraping edge. With minute retouch from under surface borer tip is produced at the shorter margin opposite to the bulbar end and at the end portion of the retouched right lateral side by careful working, fresh. (66×52×13mm)

'Y' 4. Borer cum end scraper on an irregular end flake. One of the lateral margins (right) retouched from the upper surface to obtain straight scarping edge. Borer tip produced at the end portion of the retouched lateral side by careful working fresh. (50×45×16mm)

'O' 1. Thick oval shaped levallois end flake of Brown Quartzite. Upper surface characterized by number of shallow flakes all towards centre. Under surface unworked except one or two flake scars towards bulb, with prominent bulb of percussion and faceted stroking platform, fresh. (78×59×16mm)

'O' 2. Thin rectangular flake on gray Quartzite, striking platform removed by subsequent flaking. Undersurface unworked except by removing one or two flake scars along the margin. Upper surface characterized by numerous shallow flake scars all directed towards centre, fresh. (43×36×11mm)

'O' 3. Very thin leaf shaped flake on Brown Quartzite. Faceted platform is visible. Undersurface unworked except one or two flake scars along margin. Upper surface shows number of small shallow flake scars and retouch along the periphery, fresh. (39×30×10mm)

'R' 1. Thin rectangular flake on dark gray Quartzite. Striking platform and a prominent bulb of percussion and primary flake surface on the under surface. Upper surface characterized by number of shallow flake scars all directed towards centre forming irregular median ridge; fresh (47×34×11mm)

'R' 2. Thick rectangular flake blade on gray Quartzite, striking platform partly removed. Undersurface unworked with a prominent bulb of percussion and is main flake surface. Upper surface shows a median ridge longitudinally with shallow long flake scars on either side. Retouched, slightly broken, fresh. (42×27×13mm)

'R' 3. Thin leaf shaped flake blade on Brown Quartzite prepared platform (striking). Platform is removed by subsequent flaking, bulbar scar prominent. Undersurface unworked upper surface characterized by three shallow flake scars; forming three irregular ridges, used marks visible along the margins, fresh. (62×38×14mm)

'R' 4. (Central piece) Levellois core of dark Brown Quartzite, number of shallow flake scars all directed towards a deep small flake scar; the other surface is fully flaked by number of small shallow flakes, fresh. (65×56×28cm)

Plate XII

Assemblage of Standardized Tool Types

LEFT SIDE COMPARTMENT	RIGHT SIDE COMPARTMENT		
Left top Diamond 1,1a. Side Scrapers Left middle Rectangle 2. Double Edged Scraper Left bottom Diamond 3,3a. Side-Cum-End Scraper Middle top Square 4. Side-Cum-End Scrapers Right top Diamond 5,5a. End Scrapers Right Middle Rectangle 6. Scraper Cum Borer 6a. Scraper On Flake Right bottom Diamond 7. Side scraper 7a. Double Edged Side Scraper Middle bottom Square 8. Borer Centre left bottom Diamond 9. Hollow Cum End Scraper 9a. Scraper Centre left top Diamond 10. Leaf Shaped End Flake 10a. Parallel Sided Flake Centre right top Diamond 11. Levellois Core 11a.Flake Centre right bottom Diamond 12,12a. Points Centre Diamond 13. Scraper	Left Top Circle 1. Scraper 2. Side Cum End Scraper 3. Scraper on Flake 4. Borer Cum Scraper Left Middle Circle 5. Side Scraper 6. Scraper 7,8 Side Cum End Scraper Left Bottom Circle 9. Side Scraper 10.Scraper 11.End Scraper 12.Borer Cum Scraper	Middle Top Square 13.End Flake 14.Side Cum End Scraper 15.Round Scraper 16.Convex Scraper 17.Conical Core Middle Bottom Square 18.Side Scraper 19.End Scraper 20.Hollow Cum Side Scraper 21.Notched Scraper 22.Scraper on Flake	Right Top Circle 23.Side Scraper 24,25. End Scraper 26. Flake 27. Core Scraper Right Middle Circle 28. Side Scraper 29. End Scraper 30. Round Scraper 31. Borer cum Scraper 32. Leaf Shaped Point Right Bottom Circle 33. Double Edged Side Scraper 34. Round Scraper 35. Double Edged Side Cum End Scraper 36. Borer cum Scraper 37. Side Scraper

DESCRIPTION OF LEFT SIDE COMPARTMENT

LEFT TOP DIAMOND

1. (YLM) Side scraper : Parallel shaped broken end flake of Brown Quartzite, upper surface primary and bulb is removed, one of the lateral margins retouched on the upper surface, fresh. (70×53×25mm)

1a. (YLM) Side scraper on thick end flake of Brown Quartzite. Upper surface flaked with two median ridges. Under surface is primary. One of the lateral margins retouched mainly on upper surface to obtain convex and straight scraping edge, fresh. (75×35×20mm)

LEFT MIDDLE RECTANGLE

2. (YLM) Double edged side scraper on a long and thick barrel shaped flake, opposite lateral margins retouched in both faces to form convex scraping edges, under surface is primary, upper surface fully flaked and shows many ridges, fresh. (125×75×25mm)

LEFT BOTTOM DIAMOND

3. (YLM) Side cum end scraper on irregular shaped end flake of pale gray Quartzite. Upper surface is fully flaked with many irregular ridges, one of the longest lateral margins and one of the shorter margin opposite to bulbar end is retouched mainly on upper surface; fresh. (94×53×27mm)

3a.(YLM) Side cum end scraper on roughly triangular shaped end flake of pale gray Quartzite, upper surface is fully flaked. Under surface is primary. Retouch is made on both the lateral margins and opposite to bulbar end from both the faces to form convex scraping edges; fresh. (69×54×24mm)

MIDDLE TOP SQUARE

4. (YLM) Side cum end scraper on a thick end flake of dark gray Quartzite. Upper surface is fully flaked with two median parallel sided ridges and is thick at the centre as well as at the bulbar end (thin at the working end), tapers at the working end and along the longer lateral margins. Retouch is made, on the upper surface and also on the under surface. Under surface is flaked with a prominent bulb, semi rolled. (90×58×36mm)

RIGHT TOP DIAMOND

5. (YLM) End scraper on irregular end flake. Upper surface is fully flaked with irregular ridges. The opposite margin of bulbar end is steeply retouched to obtain straight scraping edge. Under surface is primary, fresh. (60×45×19mm)

5a. (YLM) Side cum end scraper on roughly triangular end flake of dark Brown

Quartzite, upper surface is flaked. Retouch is made on the broader margin, that is opposite to bulbar end from under surface and also on both the lateral margins. Under surface is primary, fresh. (60×45×12mm)

RIGHT MIDDLE RECTANGLE

6. (YLM) Scraper- cum -borer on a thick squarish end flake of grey Quartzite. One of the lateral margins is retouched from under surface. Other longer side is thick for handhold. Borer tip is produced at the end portion of the retouched lateral side by careful working, fresh. (95×95×40mm)

6a. (YLM) Scraper on an end flake of Grey Quartzite, upper surface shows a median high ridge towards right side with a large and small, deep and shallow flake scars. Scraping edge is produced on one of the longer axis by steep retouch on the upper surface. Under surface is primary with a bulb of percussion.

RIGHT BOTTOM DIAMOND

7. (YLM) Side scraper on end flake of Brown Quartzite. One of the longer lateral margins is sloppy and the other longer side is high and thick with irregular margin for handhold, fresh. (70×44×24mm)

7a. (YLM) Double edged scraper on a thick side flake, upper surface is fully flaked with two longitudinal margins, under surface is primary. Retouch is made on both the longer lateral margins on upper surface to obtain straight scarping edge, fresh. (81×50×24mm)

MIDDLE BOTTOM SQUARE

8. (YLM) Borer on thick rectangular end flake of Brown Quartzite. Thick significant projecting point made by removal of flakes from tip portion. Tip trimmed on upper surface; Upper surface fully flaked with irregular ridges and, shallow and deep flakes of different dimensions; under surface is primary, fresh. (91×51×30mm)

CENTRE LEFT BOTTOM DIAMOND

9. (YLM) Hollow-cum-end scraper on a rectangular flake of Brown Quartzite, upper surface shows slight patination towards the working end. Shallow longitudinal flakes are removed by step flaking on one of the longer margin. Hollow is made by retouch inside it. The margin opposite to the bulbar end is also retouched by step flaking on the upper surface. The under surface shows two small and large shallow flake scars and a deep flake scar with an irregular ridge. Semi rolled. (60×47×23mm)

9a. (YLM) Scraper on a small thick end flake of dark Brown Quartzite, one of the longer lateral margins shows a notch and the opposite longer lateral margin is retouched son the upper surface, under surface is primary. Upper surface shows a forked median ridge with long shallow flake scars. (46×30×14mm)

CENTRE LEFT TOP DIAMOND

10. (YLM) A leaf shaped end flake of Grey Quartzite with a slight brownish patina. Upper surface shows a longitudinal median ridge with long flake scars on either side. Under surface is primary flake surface and the bulb is removed. Facetted platform is also visible. Tip is slightly broken. Both the opposite longer lateral margins show secondary working, slightly rolled. (65×35×20mm)

10a. (YLM) Parallel sided, rectangular end flake of Grey Quartzite. Upper surface fully flaked with a median ridge, under surface is partly flaked with a prominent bulb of percussion, the bulb partly removed. Both the opposite larger margins show use marks, fresh. (60×40×15mm)

CENTRE RIGHT TOP DIAMOND

11. (YLM) Oval shaped Levellois core of Brown Quartzite. On one of the faces several small flakes have been removed, all directed towards the centre. Their surface is characterized by prominently large and a few flake scars, fresh. (70×60×36mm)

11a. (YLM) A medium sized thick flake on Brown Quartzite. Plain striking platform with a prominent bulb of percussion and primary under surface. Upper surface is fully flaked with a median ridge. Occasionally used marks along the periphery. Semi rolled. (50×47×15mm)

CENTRE RIGHT BOTTOM DIAMOND

12. (YLM) Point on a sub triangular end flake of Grey Quartzite. Under surface with diffused bulb and plain striking platform. Primary lateral margins mainly retouched on upper surface. Pointed tip is slightly broken and shows minute retouch. Upper surface fully flaked with a forked ridge. (88×58×28mm)

12a. (YLM) Point on thick elongated triangular shaped end flake of Grey Quartzite. Both the lateral margins show presence of tiny flake scars. Tip point is slightly broken and is retouched minutely. Upper surface is fully flaked with ridges. Under surface is partly flaked extending up to the ¾th of the tool i.e., the bulbar end and bulb removed. (64×50×15mm)

CENTRE DIAMOND

13. (YLM) Scraper on a disc shaped core on a brown Cherty Quartzite. Under surface shows shallow and deep flake scars, upper surface is steeply flaked retaining a patch of cortex at the centre. Convex scraping edge extends ¾th of the periphery by steep flaking on the upper surface, fresh. (80×70×42mm)

RIGHT SIDE COMPARTMENT

LEFT TOP CIRCLE

1. (KPM) Scraper on a thick roughly rectangular end flake of Grey Quartzite. Under surface primary with a prominent bulb which is partly removed. Plain striking platform, upper surface shows a central large rectangular deep flake scar surrounded by a small shallow flake scar all along the periphery. Steeply retouched except at the bulbar end and also a notch is produced on the right lateral longer margin, minutely flaked inside the notch, fresh. (89×65×28mm)

2. (KPM) Side-cum-end scraper on a nut shaped flake of Grey Quartzite with a slight brown patina, under surface is primary with prepared striking platform; upper surface shows a median longitudinal ridge. Retouch is made on the margin opposite to bulbar end from both the surfaces. The lateral margins show use marks, semi rolled. (66×58×23mm)

3. (KPM) Scraper on an irregular flake of Grey Quartzite, under surface is primary with a prominent bulb and a plain striking platform. Upper surface is partly flaked with thick sides. A notch is produced on the longer margin opposite to the bulbar end. Minutely retouched inside the notch on the under surface. Retouch is also made on parts of both the lateral margins on the upper surface, semi rolled. (75×64×22mm)

4. (KPM) Borer-cum-scraper on small rectangular broken end flake of Grey Quartzite. Under surface is primary and bulb is partly removed. Upper surface is fully flaked. Thin significant projecting point is made by the removal of flakes from tip portion. Tip trimmed on upper surface. Both the longer and lateral margins are steeply retouched to obtain scraping edge from upper surface, fresh. (50×39×17mm)

LEFT MIDDLE CIRCLE

5. (GVP) Side scraper on a sub triangular end flake of Brown Quartzite. Under surface is primary with bulbar scar and prepared striking platform. Upper surface flaked with forked ridge. Deep flake scars are removed along the right lateral margin to obtain a sharp cutting edge. Further, retouch is made by step flaking on the same margin to obtain scraping edge, fresh. (92×72×32mm)

6. (GVP) Scraper on a thick dark Brown Quartzite on a rectangular shaped flake. Both the surfaces show median high ridge with sloppy lateral margins. Both the lateral margins are steeply worked on one surface to obtain scraping edge. Semi rolled. (90×54×32mm)

7. (GVP) Side cum end scraper on a thick rectangular flake of Brown Quartzite. Under surface is primary, with a bulbar scar and plain striking platform. Upper surface is fully flaked leaving a patch of cortex at the tip. One of the long lateral margins,

opposite to the bulbar end are steeply retouched to obtain straight scraping edge, fresh. (98×84×29mm)

8. (GVP) Side cum end scraper on a triangular end flake of Brown Quartzite. Under surface is primary with diffused bulb and plain striking platform. Upper surface with a parallel-sided high ridge towards the right half, is with long and deep flake scars. Retouch is made on the right lateral margin, on the margin opposite to the bulbar end and also on the upper surface to obtain slight scraping edge. (86×61×26mm)

LEFT BOTTOM CIRCLE

9. (GDA) Side scraper on a roughly end flake of Grey Quartzite. Upper surface shows a forked median high ridge towards the right half with large and small, deep and shallow flake scars on the left side. Scraping edge is obtained on the left lateral longer margin by steep retouch on the upper surface. Under surface is primary, with a diffused bulb of percussion and a plain striking platform, fresh. (88×44×23mm)

10. (GDA) A scraper on thick and broad roughly rectangular flake of fine grained Quartz of pale Grey colour. Under surface is primary with a bulb of percussion and plain striking platform. Upper surface is fully flaked with forked median ridge. Retouch is made on both the opposite margins of the upper surface extending to the tip. Semi rolled. (100×72×27mm)

11. (GDA) End scraper on a roughly triangular thick flake of coarse-grained White Quartz. Under surface is primary with plain striking platform. Bulb diffused. The margin opposite to the bulbar end is slightly narrowing and shows retouch on the upper surface to obtain straight striking edge. Semi rolled. (83×60×19mm)

12. (GDA) Borer -cum -scraper on a thick end flake of whitish fine grained Quartz with a slight brown patina all over the surface. Under surface is primary with two bulbs and prepared striking platform. Upper surface is fully flaked. Thick significant projecting point is made by the removal of flakes from the tip portion. Tip is trimmed on upper surface, fresh. (83×70×42mm)

MIDDLE TOP SQUARE

13. (AMBD) Roughly triangular shaped end flake of dark Brown Quartzite, upper surface shows a series of small flake scars, under surface shows primary flaking with diffused bulb of percussion and a prepared striking platform. The retouch is made along the periphery, fresh. (70×60×23mm)

14. (AMBD) Side cum end scraper on an irregular end flake of Brown Quartzite. Broader margin opposite to bulbar end is steeply retouched on the upper surface. The

left lateral margin is retouched on the under surface to obtain scraping edge. Under surface is primary with a bulbar scar and a prepared striking platform. Upper surface shows small and large shallow and deep flake scars, fresh. (85×50×25mm)

15. (AMBD) A round scraper on a roughly rectangular end flake. Upper surface shows shallow large flake scars on the right half and a series of very small step flaking on the left half of the specimen. Retouch is made all along the periphery except at the bulbar end. Under surface is primary with a prominent bulb and a plain striking platform, fresh. (52×44×20mm)

16. (AMBD) A convex scraper on a sub-triangular thick flake of Brown Quartzite. Upper surface shows irregular high ridge with shallow flake scars. Under surface is primary with a bulbar scar. Scraping edge is obtained all along the periphery by steep flaking from upper surface and occasionally on the under surface. Fresh. (54×36×20mm)

17. (AMBD) Fragment of a small flake in conical shape having a flat under surface. Upper surface shows shallow longitudinal flake scars. It retains a patch of cortex on one side, fresh. (64×50×34mm)

MIDDLE BOTTOM SQUARE

18. Side Scraper 19. End Scraper 20. Hollow cum Side Scraper

21. Notched Scraper 22. Scraper on Flake

RIGHT TOP CIRCLE

23. (DPD) A side scraper on a small rectangular thin flake. The left lateral margin is steeply retouched on upper surface. Under surface is primary with a diffused bulb and prepared striking platform. Semi rolled. (50×47×11mm)

24. (DPD) End cum notched scraper on an irregular end flake of Brown Quartzite. The broader margin opposite to the bulbar end is steeply retouched on the upper surface to obtain scraping edge. One of the lateral margins shows small notch with minimum working inside, fresh. (70×54×16mm)

25. End scraper on a roughly rectangular flake. Upper surface is fully flaked. Retouch is made on the margin opposite to the bulbar end on upper surface. Under surface is primary with a prominent bulb and prepared striking platform, fresh. (55×45×18mm)

26. (DPD) A small triangular end flake with a pointed tip. Upper surface shows three irregular long flakes with low parallel ridges. Under surface primary with a

prominent bulb and prepared striking platform. Use marks are noticeable on the periphery. Semi rolled. (75×60×19mm)

27. Core Scraper

RIGHT MIDLLE CIRCLE

28. (RPL) Side scraper on a roughly rectangular thick end flake of Cherty Quartzite. Upper surface shows a median irregular high ridge with shallow and deep flake scars on either side. Left lateral margin is steeply retouched to obtain scraping edge. Under surface is primary with a prepared striking platform. Semi rolled. (62×47×23mm)

29. (RPL) End scraper on an irregular end flake of Chert. Upper surface fully flaked, steep working is done on the margin opposite to the bulbar end from under surface. Under surface is primary with a prominent bulb of percussion and prepared striking platform. Semi rolled. (58×36×13mm)

30. (RPL) Round scraper on a thick end flake. Upper surface is fully flaked with small shallow flake scars. Under surface is partly flaked with a bulb of percussion and prepared striking platform. Retouch is made steeply all along the periphery. Semi rolled. (54×46×16mm)

31. (RPL) Borer cum scraper on a small thick rectangular end flake of Cherty Quartzite. Upper surface shows a median forked ridge. Under surface primary with a small bulb and plain striking platform. Retouch is made on the right lateral margin on the under surface. Borer point is obtained on the margin opposite to the bulbar end. Tip is minutely retouched. Semi rolled. (35×33×10mm)

32. (RPL) A leaf shaped point on a side flake of a brownish Cherty Quartzite. Upper surface shows a median high ridge with few small flake scars. Under surface primary with a small bulb and prepared striking platform. Both the longer lateral margins are retouched. They converge into a point at the tip. Semi rolled. (60×33×15mm)

RIGHT BOTTOM CIRCLE

33. (MTJPR) Double edged side scraper on a broken rectangular end flake of Cherty Quartzite. Upper surface shows median high ridge towards the left half of the specimen with shallow and deep flake scars. Under surface is primary with bulbar scar and striking platform. Both the margins are steeply retouched, one from the upper surface and other from the under surface, fresh. (58×40×18mm)

34. Round Scraper 35. Double Edged Side Cum End Scraper 36. Borer cum Scraper

37. Side Scraper

REFERENCES

Sankalia, H. D. 1964 *Stone Age Tools Their Techniques, Names and Probable Functions,* Deccan College, Pune.

Sen, D. 1966 *The Soanian and the Pebble Tool Complex,* "Man in India", Vol.40 No.3, pp. 178-191.

Allchin, B. & R. 1968 *The Birth of Indian Civilization.*

Foote, R. B. 1916 Prehistoric and Protohistoric Antiquities Of India.

Isaac, N. 1960 *The Stone Age Cultures of Kurnool,* Ph.D., Thesis, Pune Univ. & Deccan College libraries.

Krishna Swamy, V. D. 1951 & Soundara Rajan K.V. *The Lithic Tool Industries of the Singrauli & Basin* Ancient India No.12.

Mishra, V. N. 1962 *The Stone Age Cultures of Rajasthan,* Ph.D., Thesis Deccan College Pune.

Murthy, M. L. K. 1966 *The Stone Age Cultures of Chittor,* Ph.D.,Thesis Deccan College Pune.

Rao, S. N. 1966 *The Stone Age Cultures of Nalgonda,* Ph.D., Thesis Deccan College Pune

Timma Reddy, K. 1968 *Prehistory of Cuddapah* Ph.D., Thesis Deccan College Pune.

Soundara Rajan, K. V. 1950 *Studies in Stone Ages of Nagarjuna Konda and it's Neighbourhood* Ancient India No.14, pp. 49-113.

Paddaiah, K. 1968 *Pre and Protohistoric Investigation in Sorapoor Doab,* Ph. D., Thesis, Deccan College, Pune.

Chapter—V

Upper Palaeolithic Period (30,000-8,000 B.P.)

The Upper Palaeolithic as a separate cultural phase in Indian Prehistory has been recognised (Sankalia 1974) Thaper 1974-76) as a result of researches spread over the last 20 years Andhra Pradesh; (R.B. And H. B Foote in 1844; Cammiade and Burkatt 1930; Soundara Rajan 1958; Isaac, N. 1960; S. N. Rao 1966; M. L. K. Murthy 1968, 1974,1979; Timma reddy 1970; M. L. K. Murthy and Timma Reddy 1976 and Kasturi Bai 1982); Madras: (K. V. Raman 1960-61; Vedula Jaiswal); Karnataka; (B. Subba Rao 1963;Sheshadri 1964; Paddaiah 1970; Pappu 1972); Maharashtra: (K. R. V. Todd; Malik 1956; Corvinus 1960; Sankalia 1956, 1974; S. A. Sali 1973-74; R. V. Joshi and Team 1975-76; Srinivasan); Gujarat: (Allchin & Goudia 1971-72); Rajasthan; (Bridgit Allchin 1972); Madhya Pradesh: (Wakankar 1957, Mishra 1977); Uttar Pradesh : (G.R.Sarma 1956-57,1975); Bihar : (A. K. Ghosh 1965-66, 1970) and Assam: (Sarma 1974).

Upper Palaeolithic sites are now known to spread widely in the country from Ganga basin in the North to Tamilnadu in the South and from Assam in the east to Gujarat, Rajasthan in the West. There are broad typo-technological similarities among these disparate groups of assemblages so that, they may all be brought under one head, the Upper Palaeolithic. However chronological considerations need to take into account regional variations.

On typological considerations it has been assigned to late Pleistocene and early Holocene.

The available carbon 14 dates indicate that the Upper Palaeolithic cultures flourished in India from about 20,000 to 10,000 years ago (Patne 1979-80 Asla). With in this time bracket, the industries must have evolved. The evolution of the industries in reference to the time scale as well as the regional variations noticeable in artifactual compositions make the upper Palaeolithic a complex and fascinating area of study.

Plate XIII

Assemblage of Tool Types in Changed Environment

LEFT COMPARTMENT	
Left Top Inverted 'L' Board	Right Top Inverted 'L' Board
1. Side Scraper	7,8,9,10. Side Cum End Scrapers
2. Scraper	11,12. Notched Scrapers
3. Double Side Scraper	13,14. Borrer Cum Scrapers
4. Double edged Scraper	Right Bottom Inverted 'L' Board
5. End Scraper on Blade	15. Symmetric Point
6. End Scraper on Flake	16,17. Burines
Left Bottom 'L' Board	18. Lunate
23,24,28. Retouched Blades	19,20,21,22. Backed Blades
'T' Board	Inverted 'T' Board
29. Parallel Sided Blade	32,33. Blades
30. Broken Blade	34. Fluted Core
31. Core	

CENTRE 'U' BOARD	
1,2. Side Scrapers	11,12. Borrer Cum Scrapers
3,4. Double Side Scrapers	13,14,15,16. Backed Blades
5. End Scraper	17. Lunate
6. Convex Scraper	18,19. Burines
7. Core Scraper	20,21,24,25. Retouched Blades
8. Round Scraper	22,23. Broken Blades
9. Side Cum Notched Scraper	26,27. Points On Flake
10. Side Cum Hollow Scraper	28,29. Core rejuvenated flake

RIGHT COMPARTMENT	
Left Top 'L' Board	22,23,24. Blades
1,2. Double Side Scraper	'T' Board
3. End Scraper	25,26,27. Blades
4. Side Cum End Scraper	Right Top Inverted 'L' Board
5. Hollow Cum Side Scraper	7,8. Notched Scrapers
6. Notched Scraper	9. Core Scraper
Left Bottom Inverted 'L' Board	10. Round Scraper
19,20. Blades	11. Borer cum Scraper
21.Retouched Blades	12. Point on Blade

Right Bottom Inverted 'L' Board	Inverted 'T' Board
13. Knife	25, 26, 27. Blades
14,15. Backed Blades	28. Core
16. Macro Lunate	29. Flake
17,18. Burines	30. Rejuvenated flake
	31. Irregular flake

DESCRIPTION OF TOOLS IN LEFT COMPARTMENT

LEFT TOP INVERTED 'L' BOARD

1. Side scraper on thick squarish flake of brownish Grey Quartzite. Scraping edge is created on one of the lateral margins by step flaking, under surface is primary with a diffused bulb of percussion and faceted platform, fresh. (40×45×20mm)

2. Scraper on parallel sided blade of brownish Quartzite. Upper surface shows a median high ridge. Scraping edge is found on one of the lateral margins, by the removal of minute flakes from under surface. Under surface is primary. Slightly rolled. (60×35×14mm)

3. Double side scraper on a broken thick long blade of Banded Quartzite. Upper surface shows two ridges with shallow and deep flake scars. Under surface primary with bulb of percussion and facetted string platform. Both the lateral margins are steeply flaked to obtain scraping edges, fresh. (75×50×18mm)

4. Double edged side scraper on a thin broad broken blade of Brown Quartzite. Upper surface shows a long median ridge and a small irregular edge. Under surface is primary. Both the lateral margins are steeply worked from upper surface to get scraping edges, fresh. (75×54×15mm.)

5. End scraper on a thick long blade of Grey Quartzite. Upper surface shows two longitudinal parallel ridges with shallow flake scars. Under surface partly flaked on the posterior end with prominent bulb of percussion with striking platform. Postcrior end is steeply flaked to obtain scraping edge.

6. End scraper on a small squarish end flake of Brown Quartzite. Upper surface shows irregular ridges with small and deep flake scars. The broader edge opposite to the bulbar end is steeply flaked from upper surface. Under surface is primary with a prominent bulb of percussion and striking platform, fresh. (42×4×17mm)

RIGHT TOP INVERTED 'L' BOARD

7. Side cum end scraper on a side flake of Brown Quartzite. One of the lateral margins and the edge opposite to the bulbar end are steeply flaked from the upper

surface. The other lateral margin is flaked from the under surface. Under surface is primary with bulbar scar and facetted platform. (65×41×14mm)

8. Side cum end scraper on a broken blade of Brown Quartzite. Upper surface shows a high median ridge forking at the end. Under surface is primary with a deep bulbar scar. The lateral margin and the margin opposite to the bulbar end are steeply flaked to obtain scraping edge from the upper surface. Semi rolled. (50×34×14mm)

9. Side cum end scraper on a thick flake blade of Grey Quartzite. Upper surface shows a high median ridge with shallow and deep, small flake scars. The scraping edge is found on both lateral margins and at the posterior end by steep flaking from the upper surface, fresh. (74×44×17mm.)

10. Side cum end scraper on a thick blade of Brown Quartzite. Upper surface shows a long median high ridge with two irregular ridges on either side. Under surface primary with a prominent bulb of percussion and thick striking platform. Steep flaking is visible all along the periphery except at the bulbar end, fresh. (50×25×20mm)

11. Notched scraper on a long flake blade of Quartzite. One of the lateral margins shows steep flaking from upper surface. The other lateral margin which is irregular shows a notch created from the under surface. Under surface is primary with a bulb of percussion and striking platform, fresh. (88×57×17mm)

12. Notched scraper on an end flake blade of Grey Quartzite. Upper surface is with irregular median ridge and with large, shallow, small and deep flake scars. Under surface is primary with a prominent bulb of percussion and striking platform. One of the long lateral margins shows steep flaking on upper surface to obtain convex scraping edge. The other lateral surface shows a notch near the bulbar end produced from the under surface, fresh. (77×40×21mm)

13. Borer cum scraper on a thick long flake blade of round Quartzite. Upper surface shows two longitudinal high ridges with shallow long and small flake scars. Under surface is primary with a prominent bulb of percussion and facetted striking platform. Borer end is obtained on the margin opposite to the bulbar end with minute secondary working on either side of the borer point. The right lateral margin is steeply worked to obtain a straight scraping edge. Semi rolled. (88×46×28mm)

14. Borer cum scraper on a thick parallel sided blade of Grey Quartzite. Upper surface shows a median high longitudinal ridge with two low ridges on either side of it. Under surface primary with a bulbar scar and faceted striking platform. Steep flaking is visible all along the periphery except at the bulbar end. Borer point is found on the diffuse end with minute working on either side of the tip, fresh. (68×35×17mm)

RIGHT BOTTOM INVERTED 'L' BOARD

15. Symmetrical point on a small thick flake blade of Grey Quartzite. Upper surface shows many low ridges with small shallow flake scars. Under surface is primary with a prominent bulb of percussion. Both the lateral margins show retouch converging into a point at the posterior end. Semi rolled. (38×19×5mm)

16. Burin on an irregular end flake of dark Brown Quartzite. On the elongated right lateral margin which converging with the diffuse end, a burin tip is obtained by the removal on either side. Fresh. (46×26×9mm)

17. Burin cum backed piece on a parallel-sided blade of Brown Quartzite. Upper surface shows long parallel sides and two ridges with long shallow flake scars. Under surface. Along one of the margins a linear spall is removed to obtain burin tip.

18. (YLM 40) Macro-Lunate on a crescent shaped thick end flake of Brown Quartzite. The arc with partly blunting is visible, followed by removal of a large angular flake to obtain. The arc is obtained by blunting on the right margin, while the left margin is with the natural backing. The working edge possesses retouch. (48×34×19mm)

19. (YLM) Backed blade on thick broken blade of dark Brown Quartzite, upper surface shows a forked high ridge occupying the extreme right half and sloping towards the left side into a sharp edge which is retouched. The right side margin shows blunting for handhold, under surface primary with prepared striking platform, fresh. (43×27×10mm)

20. (YLM) Backed blade on a thick elongated narrow long blade of Brown Quartzite. Upper surface shows two parallel-sided ridges with shallow large and small flake scars. The longitudinal left margin is thick and partly blunted while the right lateral margin slopes from the upper surface to a sharp cutting edge with a retouch. Under surface is primary with a diffuse bulb of percussion, fresh. (55×18×15mm)

21. (YLM) Backed blade on a thick flake blade of Brown Quartzite, upper surface shows a median high ridge forked towards bulbar end and another parallel ridge at the extreme right side with large, shallow deep flake scar. The left lateral margin is thick blunted by secondary working, which extends to posterior end. The right lateral margin is sloping, to a sharp cutting edge, which shows minute retouch for cutting purpose, fresh. (64×37×21mm)

22. (YLM) Backed blade on slightly broken blade of dark Brown Quartzite. Upper surface shows median ridge extending to either ends, with a long shallow flake on the right half of the surface, thick at the centre thins down for cutting on purpose on the right lateral margin which shows minute retouch. The left lateral margin is thick and blunted. Under surface is primary with a bulb of percussion and a striking platform, fresh. (77×33×16mm)

LEFT BOTTOM 'L' BOARD

23. (YLM) Retouched blade on Grey Quartzite. Upper surface shows a high median ridge. Under surface is primary with a prominent bulb of percussion, a faceted striking platform and is retouched on either of the lateral margins. There is a clear cut attempt for the preparation of a tang on the bulbar end by the removal of a long flake on either side followed by minute work for hafting, fresh. (93×50×21mm)

24. (YLM) A thick retouched blade of Brown Quartzite. Upper surface shows a high median ridge forked on either ends, with large and shallow flake scars thick at the centre and slopes on the lateral margins which are retouched. Under surface is primary with a bulbar scar and faceted striking platform, fresh. (99×39×21mm)

25. (YLM) Slightly broken retouched flake blade of Grey Quartzite, upper surface shows two parallel-sided ridges with a deep flake scar in between. The lateral margins are retouched. Under surface primary with a striking platform, fresh. (63×41×14mm)

26. (YLM) Partly broken retouched blade of Brown Quartzite. Broken at the tip upper surface shows a median ridge forked towards bulbar end. Both the lateral margins are retouched. Under surface primary with a bulbar scar, fresh. (49×31×14mm)

27. (YLM) Partly broke retouched blade of Grey Quartzite. Upper surface shows a median ridge with large and small shallow and deep flake scars. Under surface primary with bulbar scar and faceted striking platform. Both the lateral margins are discontinuously retouched, fresh. (61×44×14mm)

28. (YLM) Partly broke retouched blade of Brown Quartzite. Upper surface shows median high ridge with a shallow large flake scars on either side. Under surface is primary with plain striking platform. Retouched on either lateral margins on the under surface, fresh. (58×36×13mm)

'T' BOARD

29. (YLM) A parallel sided thick flake blade of Brown Quartzite. Upper surface shows irregular high ridges on the left half of the flake. Right half shows shallow and deep, small flake scars under surface primary with a bulb of percussion. The distal end shows secondary working for scraping, fresh. (60×38×16mm)

30. (YLM) Thick broken blade of Brown Quartzite. A median high ridge on the upper surface. Under surface primary with a striking platform, retouched lateral long margins on the under surface. A partial retouch on the upper surface on the distal end, fresh. (67×33×15mm)

31. (YLM) A half broken conical core of Brown Quartzite. A patch of cortex retained on the upper surface. These irregular flutations are visible. Steep flakes are removed on one large lateral margin for scraping, fresh. (100×89×46mm)

INVERTED 'T' BOARD

32. (YLM) Flake blade on a Grey Quartzite. Upper surface shows a median ridge forked on either sides. Use marks on either margins. Under surface primary with a prominent bulb of percussion with a prepared striking platform, fresh. (79×41×13mm)

33. (YLM) Flake blade of Grey Quartzite, upper surface shows a forked ridge on the left half of the tool, with small shallow and deep flake scars and large shallow flakes scar on the right half of the flake. Under surface primary with a prominent bulb of percussion and prepared striking platform. Use marks on either lateral margin, fresh. (54×39×13mm)

34. A conical fluted core of dark Brown Quartzite, large irregular flutations along the circumference leaving a part of the surface, flat large prepared platform, fresh. (120×88×54mm)

CENTRE 'U' BOARD

1. (GDA) Side scraper on a squarish flake blade of Brown Quartzite, right lateral margin steeply normal to obtain scraping edge, under surface partly flaked, bulbous force. Upper surface flaked with shallow small flake scars, fresh. (50×39×17mm)

2. (GDA) Side scraper on a thick side flake of dark Brown Quartzite. Undersurface flaked along the margins with a bulb. Upper surface with a median high ridge with shallow and deep flake scars. Scraping edge obtained on the right lateral margin by steep flaking on the under surface, fresh. (63×45×23mm)

3. (GDA) Double side scraper on a flake blade of Brown Quartzite. Upper surface shows three parallel ridges with shallow long flake scars in between. Under surface is partly flaked along one of the margins and at the distal end, with two bulbar scars one inside the other. Both the longer margins are steeply worked to obtain straight scraping edges, fresh. (84×44×16mm)

4. (GDA) Double side scraper on a thick dark brown flake blade of Quartzite. Upper surface with a high median ridge with shallow long and small flake scars. Under surface is primary except along one of the lateral margin with a diffused bulb of percussion. Right lateral margin is steeply worked to obtain straight scraping edge. Left lateral margin steeply flaked on under surface and occasionally upper surface to obtain convex scraping edge, fresh. (74×45×21mm)

5. (GDA) End scraper on a flake blade of Brown Quartzite. Upper surface shows two long median ridges with shallow small and long flake scars. Under surface is primary with a bulb of percussion and a bulbar scar. Steep flaking at the distal end to obtain scraping edge, fresh. (61×31×16mm)

6. (GDA) Convex scraper on small end flake of Brown Quartzite. Upper surface

shows three parallel longitudinal ridges, with shallow flake scars. Under surface is primary. Both the lateral margins and at the distal end are steeply flaked to obtain convex scraping edge, fresh. (46×36×17mm)

7. (GDA) Core scraper on a small oval flake core of a pebble of Brown Quartzite. One of the surfaces fully flaked with small shallow and deep flake scars, the other surface is partly flaked. Convex scraping edge is obtained all along the periphery by steep flaking, fresh. (50×46×23mm)

8. (GDA) Round scraper on a thick flake of dark Brown Quartzite. Upper surface shows a deep flake scar extending from proximal end to the centre surrounded by shallow small flake scars. Under surface primary, with a diffused bulb of percussion, scraping edge is obtained all along the periphery by steep flaking, fresh. (43×40×18mm)

9. (GDA) Side cum notched scraper on a broken blade of Brown Quartzite. Upper surface shows a long median ridge forked at the proximal end and a small ridge on the right half of the flake near the distal end where a notch is produced by removal of long flake followed by minute flaking inside the notch on the right lateral margin. Left lateral margin is steeply flaked on the upper surface to obtain scraping edge, semi worked. (82×48×16mm)

10. (GDA) Side cum hollow scraper on a broken flake blade of dark Brown Quartzite. Upper surface shows two parallel ridges wide apart with a long shallow flake scar in the centre. Under surface is primary with a bulbar scar, right lateral margin is steeply worked to obtain scraping edge, left lateral margin shows steep working at the proximal end and a hollow is produced at the distal end by the removal of a large flake followed by minute working, fresh. (71×33×13mm)

11. (GDA) Borer cum scraper on a broken side flake of Brown Quartzite. Upper surface shows a high median ridge forked at the proximal end with two shallow and one deep flake scar. Both the lateral margins are steeply flaked to obtain scraping edge. Borer end is obtained at the distal end by minute working on either side of the borer tip which is formed by left lateral margin and the distal end, fresh. (48×38×15mm)

12. (GDA) Borer cum scraper on a flake of Brown Quartzite. Upper surface shows many irregular ridges with many small shallow flake scars. Under surface partly flaked only along the margins. The left lateral margin and a part of right lateral margins are steeply worked to obtain scraping edge. Borer point is obtained at the distal end by minute working on the left margin and a part of the distal end which forms the borer tip, fresh. (62×41×18mm)

13. (GDA) Backed blade on a thick blade of dark Brown Quartzite. Upper surface shows a high median ridge with shallow and deep flake scars. Under surface is primary

with a bulbar scar, the right lateral margin is thick with a facet (one longitudinal flake is removed) acting as back, the left lateral margin made thin and minutely worked to get sharp cutting edge, fresh. (63×38×14mm)

14. (GDA) Broken backed blade on a blade of dark Brown Quartzite. Upper surface shows small and large shallow flake scars, under surface primary with a bulb of percussion. The right lateral margin shows blunting and the left lateral margin with minute secondary working for cutting purpose, fresh. (50×26×13mm)

15. (GDA) Backed blade on a broken blade of Brown Quartzite. Upper surface shows a median ridge, under surface primary. The right lateral margin is blunted to obtain back. The left lateral margin is minutely worked on the under surface for cutting, fresh. (74×39×18mm).

16. (GDA) Backed blade on a flake. Upper surface shows a large shallow flake scar in the centre with a forked ridge on the left half of the flake. Under surface primary with a bulb of percussion right side margin is untouched to act as backing. The left lateral margin is minutely worked to obtain cutting edge, fresh. (63×38×14mm)

17. (GDA) Lunate on a flake of Brown Quartzite. Upper surface shows a median ridge. The right lateral margin is convex and shows blunting. The left lateral margin shows use-marks, under surface primary with a prominent bulb of percussion, fresh. (49×35×14mm)

18. (GDA) Burin on a small blade of Brown Quartzite, upper surface shows two ridges uniting at the proximal end, under surface primary with unfacetted striking platform. One spall is removed at the distal end on the right side to obtain a basal point and the left margin is minutely blunted, fresh. (44×29×11mm)

19. (GDA) Burin on a broken blade of Brown Quartzite, upper surface shows shallow small flake scars, under surface shows partly flaked with a faceted striking platform. One vertical flake is removed on the left lateral margin at the proximal end to obtain burin facet, fresh. (40×39×13mm)

20. (GDA) Retouched blade on a broken blade of dark Brown Quartzite. Upper surface shows a median high ridge forked at the proximal end. Under surface primary with a prominent bulb of percussion and a faceted striking platform. The left lateral margin is minutely worked at the distal end, fresh. (57×25×11mm)

21. (GDA) Retouched blade on a flake blade of dark Brown Quartzite. Upper surface shows a central ridge forked at the proximal end with a large shallow, deep flake scars on either side of the ridge. Both the lateral margins are minutely retouched. Under surface is primary with a bulb of percussion and a bulbar scar, fresh. (17×38×13mm)

22. (GDA) Broken blade of Brown Quartzite. Upper surface shows two ridges

wide apart and uniting at the distal end with shallow flake scar. Under surface primary with a prominent bulb, bulbar scar and faceted striking platform. Use marks are visible on both the lateral margins, fresh. (67×57×16mm)

23. (GDA) Broken blade of Brown Quartzite. Upper surface shows two parallel ridges with a longitudinal shallow flake scar. Under surface is primary with a prominent bulb of percussion. Use marks on both the margins, fresh. (38×32×9mm)

24. (GDA) Retouched blade on Brown Quartzite. Upper surface shows two parallel ridges uniting at the distal end, surface primary with a bulb of percussion and bulbar scar and striking platform. One of the lateral margin shows minute working and the other margin use-marks, fresh. (61×35×14mm)

25. (GDA) Retouched blade of Brown Quartzite. Upper surface shows two parallel sided ridges wide apart with central longitudinal flake scar. Under surface shows primary with a bulb and bulbar scar, one of the lateral margin shows retouch and the other with use-marks, fresh. (90×32×16mm)

26. (GDA) Pointed flake on Brown Quartzite. Upper surface shows two high ridges extending from proximal to distal end forked at either end with shallow and deep flake scars. Under surface primary with a prominent bulb of percussion and faceted striking platform, fresh. (58×43×18mm)

27. (GDA) Used flake blade converting in to a point at the distal end on Brown Quartzite. Upper surface shows a median ridge with a long shallow flake scar on either side and small shallow flake scars at the proximal end. Under surface primary with a bulb and faceted striking platform, fresh. (55×30×11mm)

28. (GDA) Core rejuvenation flake on dark Brown Quartzite, broad at proximal end and narrow at the distal end and with occasional use marks along both the lateral margins. Upper surface shows median high ridge at the distal end, which bifurcates towards the proximal end and which runs wide apart. Under surface is primary, with faceted striking platform, fresh. (84×40×27mm)

29. (GDA) Core rejuvenation flake on Brown Quartzite. Thin at the proximal end and thick near the distal end. Upper surface shows irregular ridges, under surface primary with striking platform, use-marks in cribble on one of the lateral margins, fresh. (87×40×31mm)

DESCRIPTION OF TOOLS IN RIGHT COMPARTMENT

LEFT TOP 'L' BOARD

1. (GVS) Double side scraper on a flake blade of Brown Quartzite. Scrappy edge is created on both the lateral margins by steep flaking. Upper surface shows two parallel

ridges with large shallow and deep flake scar joined at the distal end; under surface primary with a bulb and bulbar seat with a faceted striking platform, fresh. (95×57×23mm)

2. (GVS) Double side scraper on a flake blade of dark Brown Quartzite, upper surface shows a central deep large flake scar followed by small shallow flake scar surrounding it. Scraping edge is obtained on both the large lateral margins, under surface primary with a prominent bulb of percussion, fresh. (68×46×16mm)

3. (GVS) End scraper on a thick flake blade of Brown Quartzite, upper surface shows two parallel high ridges on left half , and right half is sloppy. Scraping edge is obtained at the distal end by steep flaking; under surface primary with a bulb, fresh. (73×40×18mm)

4. (GVS) Side cum end scraper on a flake blade of dark Brown Quartzite. Upper surface shows a median ridge with large shallow flake scars on either side, under surface primary with a prominent bulb; steep flaking on both the lateral margins and at the distal end, fresh. (51×31×11mm)

5. (GVS) A hollow cum side scraper on an end flake of Brown Quartzite. On one of the lateral margin a hollow is obtained by removal of a large deep flake followed by minute working in side the hollow, the opposite margin which is convex with steep flaking on upper surface, under surface primary with a bulb, fresh. (66×41×21mm)

6. (GVS) A notched scraper on a dark Brown Quartzite. Flake blade on both the lateral margins towards the distal end and also a notch is created at the distal end; scraping edge is created on both the lateral margins and at the distal end, upper surface shows many irregular ridges, under surface primary with a bulb, fresh. (80×54×17mm)

RIGHT TOP INVERTED 'L' BOARD

7. (GVS) A notched scraper on irregular flake of dark Brown Quartzite, a notch is created on one of the lateral margins at the distal end, the other lateral margin shows steep flaking to obtain scraping edge, under surface primary with a bulb, fresh. (56×55×19mm)

8. (GVS) A notched scraper on a blade of Grey Quartzite. Upper surface shows a median high ridge. On one of the lateral margins a notch is produced, under surface primary with faceted striking platform, fresh. (63×23×12mm)

9. (GVS) Core scraper on a small roundish core of Brown Quartzite. Scraping edge is created on part of the periphery. (44×42×20mm)

10. (GVS) Round scraper on a ovalish flake of dark Brown Quartzite, upper surface shows small shallow flake scars, under surface primary with a bulb and faceted striking platform, scraping edge is created all along the periphery, fresh. (53×43×20mm)

11. (GVS) Borer cum scraper on irregular flake of dark Brown Quartzite, borer point is obtained at the distal end by minute working on either margin, fresh. (90×40×19mm)

12. (GVS) Point on flake blade of Brown Quartzite. Upper surface shows high median ridge, a long shallow and a long deep flake scars on either side. Under surface primary with a prominent bulb of percussion striking platform, both the lateral margins minutely worked, converge into a point at the distal end, fresh. (81×39×19mm)

RIGHT BOTTOM INVERTED 'L' BOARD

13. (GVS) Knife on a thick pointed flake blade of dark Grey Quartzite. Upper surface shows two wide parallel ridges running 3/4th of the tool and joining at the proximal and distal ends. Under surface shows primary flake surface, with a bulb of percussion and facetted striking platform; left lateral margin is thick and shows blunting and the right lateral margin shows secondary working for cutting purpose, fresh. (144×46×30mm)

14. (GVS) Backed blade of Grey Quartzite. Upper surface shows a median high ridge with long shallow ridges on either side of it followed by small shallow and deep flake scars at the proximal end. Under surface is primary, with a bulb and facetted striking platform. The left lateral margin is blunted to serve as backing and the right lateral margin is retouched to obtain sharp cutting edge; fresh. (104×41×23mm)

15. (GVS) Backed blade on a thin dark Grey Quartzite. Upper surface shows no median parallel ridges with shallow and deep scars. Under surface is primary with a diffused bulb. The right lateral margin shows retouch and the left lateral margin blunting. Fresh. (54×24×7mm)

16. (GVS) Macro Lunate on a flake of Brown Quartzite. The left lateral margin, which is thick, is partly blunted and partly flaked to serve as backing, the right lateral margin shows use-marks, fresh. (30×47×13mm)

17. (GVS) Burin on an irregular flake of Brown Quartzite. Upper surface shows small shallow and deep flake scars. Under surface is primary with a prominent bulb of percussion. Right lateral margin is thick with a shallow flake scar and left lateral margin shows removal of a vertical flake from the distal end to obtain burin spall, fresh. (55×34×20mm)

18. (GVS) Burin on a broken blade of Brown Quartzite. Upper surface shows two irregular parallel ridges uniting at the proximal end, under surface primary with a bulbar scar, left lateral margin shows use marks, right lateral margin shows two vertical spalls one below the other removal from the distal end by pressure technique to obtain burin tip, fresh. (51×41×21mm)

LEFT BOTTOM INVERTED 'L' BOARD

19. (GVS) Slightly broken flake blade on a Grey Quartzite dorsal surface shows a median high ridge forking at proximal end. Under surface is primary with a prominent bulb of percussion and a plain striking platform. Both the lateral margins show use marks, fresh. (99×50×15mm)

20. (GVS) A blade on dark Brown Quartzite, dorsal surface shows a high median ridge forking on either ends with shallow flake scars on either side. Under surface is primary with a bulb of percussion and plain striking platform. Retouched on either long margins, fresh. (73×44×19mm)

21. (GVS) Retouched blade broken at the distal end on a Brown Quartzite. Upper surface shows two parallel running ridges with long shallow flake scars in between. Under surface is primary with a prominent bulb of percussion with a facetted-striking platform. Use marks on the lateral long margins, fresh. (66×35×13mm)

22. (GVS) Parallel sided broken blade on a dark Grey Quartzite. Upper surface shows ridges with small shallow flake scars. Under surface is primary with a bulb. Right lateral margin shows minute retouch, left lateral margin with use marks, broken at the distal end, fresh. (59×24×10mm)

23. (GVS) A long broken blade on a Brown Quartzite upper surface shows high longitudinal ridge, forked towards the proximal end with shallow and deep flake scars. Under surface is primary with a prominent bulb of percussion and facetted striking platform. Both the lateral long margins show use marks, fresh. (117×50×18mm)

24. (GVS) A broken blade on a dark Brown Quartzite. Upper surface shows two parallel ridges 18mm wide apart with long shallow flake scars. Under surface is primary with a bulb and facetted platform. The left lateral margin shows minute secondary working, fresh. (91×34×13mm)

'T' BOARD

25. (GVS) A parallel sided blade on Grey Quartzite. Upper surface shows two parallel-sided ridges running irregularly and joining at the distal end. Long and small shallow and two small deep flake scars. Under surface primary with a prominent bulb and bulbar scar and with prepared striking platform. The right lateral margin shows minute retouch, fresh. (94×54×14mm)

26. (GVS) A parallel sided blade on a Brown Quartzite. Two parallel-sided ridges running wide apart with a deep flake scar at the proximal end. Under surface is primary with a striking platform. Use marks on the lateral margins. Semi rolled. (79×42×14mm)

27. (GVS) A long broad parallel sided flake blade slightly broken at the distal end. Upper surface shows a high median ridge forked on either end. Under surface is primary

with a prominent bulb of percussion. There is an attempt to reduce the width of the proximal end on left lateral margin on the under surface. Use marks are visible on either lateral margin, fresh. (124×68×24mm)

INVERTED 'T' BOARD

28. (GVS) A fragment of flake conical pebble. Core deep irregular flake scars are visible all along the surface with patches of cortex here and there, fresh. (66×53×48mm)

29. (GVS) An irregular flake of dark Brown Quartzite. Upper surface shows a median ridge forked at the proximal end with long shallow flake scar on the right half and a small shallow flake scar at the proximal end and a patch of cortex on the left half. Under surface is primary with a prominent bulb of percussion and a striking platform. Use marks are visible on the left lateral margin. (76×41×15mm)

30. (GVS) Core rejuvenation flake on Brown Quartzite. Upper surface shows a high median ridge with a series of shallow and deep flake scars on either side and at distal end. Under surface is primary with a prominent bulb of percussion and a primary striking platform, fresh. (75×35×19mm)

31. (GVS) An irregular triangular end flake on a Brown Quartzite. A median ridge forked on either end with a large flake scars on the left half of the flake. Under surface primary with a prominent bulb of percussion and faceted striking platform, fresh. (57×39×16mm)

Show Case No. 14

Tool Assemblage Types in Changed Environment Upper Palaeolithic Period

Left Top Rectangular Board	Right Top Rectangular Board
1,2 Double sided scrapers	1. Side Cum End Scrapers
3.Double sided cum end scraper	2. Side cum Hollow scraper
4.Backed Blade	3. Notched Scraper
5. End Scraper	4,5. Backed pieces
Left Middle Rectangular Board	Right Middle Rectangular Board
1.Borer cum Scraper	1.Side Cum End Scraper
2.Retouched Blade	2.Point on Flake
3.Parallel sided Blade	3,4. Retouched Blades
4.Backed Blade	5. Backed Piece
5.Retouched Blade	Right Bottom Rectangular Board
Left Bottom Rectangular Board	1.Side Scraper
1.Side cum End Scraper	2.Double Side Scraper
2.Double Side Scraper	3.End Scraper
3.Thumb Nail Scraper	4.Retouched Blade
4.Retouched Blade	5. Blade-let
5. Backed Piece	6. Double Sided Scraper

CENTRAL BOARD	
'U' 1. Side Scraper	1st Row
2. Double Side Scraper	56,57. Side Scrapers
3,4. Round Scrapers	58. Double Scraper
5. Retouched Flake	59,60,61. End Scrapers
6,7. Backed Specimens	2nd Row
'P' 8,9,12. Retouched Blades	66,67. Round Scrapers
62 to 65.Side cum End Scraper	3rd Row
10,11. Backed Pieces	68. Notched Scraper
13. Penknife	69. Side Cum End Scraper
14,15. Used flakes	70,71. Core Scrapers
'Z' 16. Macro Lunate	72. Used Blade
17. Lunate	73. Parallel Sided Blade
18. Crescent Point	4th Row
19 to 25. Backed Specimens	74,75. Parallel
26 to 35. Retouched Blades	76. Used Blade
36 to 38. Burins	77 to 79. Borer Cum Scrapers
39,40. Used Blades Sided Blades	5th Row
41,42. Parallel sided Blades	80 to 83. Used Blades
43,45,46. Used Blades	84. Flake
44. Pointed Blade	85. Retouched Point
47. Blade Point	6th Row
48, 50 to 54. Blades	86 to 88. Fluted Cores
49. Retouched Blade	

DESCRIPTION OF TOOL ASSEMBLAGE IN CHANGED ENVIRONMENT

LEFT TOP RECTANGULAR BOARD

1. (MCP) Double side scraper on a thick flake blade of Brown Quartzite. Upper surface with a median ridge extending from proximal to distal end. Under surface is partly flaked along the lateral margins and at the proximal and distal end with a prominent bulb and prepared striking platform, both the edges shows steep retouch on under surface to obtain scraping edges, fresh. (106×53×13mm)

2. (MCP) Double side scraper on a ovalish flake of pale Grey Quartzite, upper surface shows irregular ridge with shallow and deep flake scars, under surface partly flaked with shallow and deep flake scars, bulb removed, both the later edges are steeply worked to obtain scraping edge, fresh. (85×54×19mm)

3. (MCP) Double sided end scraper on a flake blade of Grey Quartzite, upper surface show a central ridge with shallow and deep small flake scars, under surface shows irregular ridge with shallow and deep flake scars. Retouch for scraping is found all along the periphery, fresh. (84×41×18mm)

4. (MCP) Backed blade on a flake blade of Brown Quartzite, upper surface fully flaked tapering towards one of the margins. The under surface is primary with bulb of percussion and bulbar scar. One of the lateral sides is thick with (natural) cortex, which serves as backing. The opposite lateral side, which is thin, shows secondary working to obtain short cutting edge, fresh. (101×43×90mm)

5. (MCP) End scraper on a thick ovalish end flake on Brown Quartzite. Upper surface shows shallow and deep flake scars, under surface is flaked along the periphery with a bulb of percussion and plain striking platform, scraping edge is obtained at the distal end partly extending to right lateral margin by steep retouch on the upper surface, fresh. (45×58×21mm)

LEFT MIDDLE RECTANGULAR BOARD

1. (KMK) Borer cum scraper on a parallel sided thick flake blade on dark Grey Quartzite, thick at the centre, tapering on all sides, upper side shows ridges converging at the centre with shallow and deep scars, under surface is primary with diffused bulb of percussion and prepared striking platform. Both the lateral margins are steeply worked to obtain scraping edge. Borer tip is obtained at the distal end and shows secondary working on either side of the borer-point, fresh. (100×41×20mm)

2. (KMK) Retouched blade on a leaf shaped specimen of Quartzite, upper surface shows high irregular ridges, the tool tapers towards the periphery with shallow and deep scars, under surface is primary with bulb of percussion and faceted striking platform. Minute secondary working is noticed on a part of the left lateral margin exhibits use-marks, tang is prepared at the proximal end by means of secondary working on either side of proximal end, fresh. (100×59×17mm)

3. (KMK) Retouched on a parallel-sided blade on a Brown Quartzite, upper surface (distal side) a forked ridge with long shallow and deep flake scars. Under surface (ventral) is primary with bulb and bulbar scars with a prepared striking platform. Left lateral margin betrays retouch while the right lateral margin shows use-marks, broken at the distal end, fresh. (74×49×10mm)

4. (VGR) Backed blade of Brown Quartzite, distal surface shows a high median ridge with a long shallow and long deep flake scars on either side of it. Ventral surface is primary with a bulb, the left lateral margin with natural cortex, the right lateral margin is thin with retouch on the ventral surface, broken at the distal end, fresh. (64×28×13mm)

5. (KMK) Retouched blade of a Grey Quartzite, distal surface shows a high median ridge forked at the proximal end with long shallow flake scars on both sides and deep small flake scar near the proximal end. Ventral surface primary with a bulb and bulbar scar and also with striking plat form, the lateral margins exhibit retouch and use-marks, fresh. (63×27×12mm)

LEFT BOTTOM RECTANGULAR BOARD

1. (SMT) Side cum end scraper on a thick blade of Brown Quartzite distal side shows a central ridge forked at distal and proximal ends with long and small shallow flake scars tapering towards margins. Under surface with a prominent bulb of percussion and thick faceted striking platform. Right lateral margin shows steep working on the distal surface extending to the distal end and the left lateral margin showing steep secondary working on the ventral surface, fresh. (69×42×16mm)

2. (KVM) Double side scraper on a flake blade of dark Brown Quartzite, distal surface shows parallel ridges joining at the distal end and ventral surface is primary with shallow bulbar scar. Both the long lateral margins show steep secondary working to obtain convex and straight scraping edges. (54×30×11mm)

3. (KPM) Thumb-nail scraper on a thick flake on an inverted 'U' shaped specimen of Brown Quartzite. Both dorsal and ventral surfaces are flaked, scraping edge is obtained all along the margin by steep flaking except at the proximal end, fresh. (43×34×16mm)

4. (SSM) Retouched blade on dark Brown Quartzite, upper surface is median ridge, forked at the proximal end with striking platform, left lateral margin shows retouch while the right lateral margin shows use-marks. Under surface is primary, broken at distal end, fresh. (59×36×11mm)

5. (PRG) Backed piece on a thick flake blade of Grey Quartzite, the right side is thick and blunt, left margin shows retouch, ventral surface is primary, fresh. (51×25×18mm)

RIGHT TOP RECTANGULAR BOARD

1. (NRK) Side cum end scraper on a thick parallel sided blade-let on Grey Quartzite. Upper surface shows high mid-ridge with long shallow flake scars, tapering on the edges. Both the lateral margins and the distal end are steeply worked to obtain straight and convex scraping edges (fresh) under side primary with a bulbar scar facetted striking platform. (44×35×13mm)

2. Side cum hollow scraper on a triangular flake of Quartzite, upper surface shows high irregular ridges with shallow and deep flake scars tapering to the margins, left later margin is steeply worked to obtain scraping edge at the distal end. A shallow and large hollow is created and followed by minute working to obtain concave scraping edge fresh. Under surface is primary with diffused bulb. (50×40×13mm)

3. (NKK) Notched scraper on a broken blade on Brown Quartzite. Upper surface shows two long parallel-sided margins with a deep flake scar in between them, under surface primary with a prominent bulb of percussion. On the left lateral margin a large notch is created on the under surface. The right lateral margin shows use marks, fresh. (67×48×18mm)

4. Backed piece on a thick leaf shaped flake on a Brown Quartzite. Upper surface shows step flaking from right to left margin, making the left margin thin and sharp for cutting purpose while the right lateral margin is thick with natural cortex serving as backing under surface primary with a bulb and striking platform. fresh. (64×48×15mm)

5. Backed piece flake blade of yellowish Brown Quartzite, thick towards the posterior end and comparatively thick at the distal end. Upper surface shows a longitudinal high margin extending from the proximal distal end on the right half of the specimen and thins down towards the left lateral margin where minute retouch is visible to serve cutting purpose. A longitudinal flake is removed on the right lateral margin to serve as backing. Under surface is primary with a bulb and a facetted striking platform. There is an attempt to prepare a tang by the removal of few deep flake scars on the left lateral margin at the distant end. (76×32×15mm)

RIGHT MIDDLE RECTANGULAR BOARD

1. (MRP) Side cum end scraper on a thumb shaped flake blade on a Grey Quartzite. Upper surface shows long shallow and small deep flake scars surrounded by deep small flake scars along the periphery. Under surface is primary with a prominent bulb of percussion and a plain striking platform. Both lateral margins and the distal end are steeply worked to obtain straight and convex scraping edges, fresh. (47×43×11mm)

2. (MRP) A point on a triangular end flake of pale Grey Quartzite, upper surface shows shallow flake scars with two ridges joining at the distal end. Under surface is primary with a bulb of diffused flake surface. Both the margins are minutely retouched converging to a point at the distal end. (41×31×11mm)

3. (MRP) A broken retouched blade on Grey Quartzite, upper surface shows a small ridge with large and shallow flake scars on either sides towards distal end, small deep flake scars towards proximal end, under surface primary with a prominent bulb of percussion and facetted striking platform. The left lateral margin shows minute retouch and the right lateral margin use-marks, fresh. (78×39×19mm)

4. (MRP) Retouched blade on pale greenish flake Quartzite. Upper surface shows two parallel ridges running wide apart longitudinally with two shallow and one deep large flake scar. Under surface primary with a prominent bulb of percussion and prepared striking platform. One of the lateral margin shows retouch and the opposite margin use marks, fresh. (71×44×17mm)

5. (MRP) Backed piece on a blade-let of pale Brown Quartzite, upper surface shows three longitudinal ridges with shallow and deep flake scars. Under surface is primary, with a prominent bulb. Right lateral margin is thick and shows removal of longitudinal flake towards entire length while the left lateral margin is thin and shows retouch to serve cutting, fresh. (51×40×14mm)

RIGHT BOTTOM RECTANGULAR BOARD

1. (YPL) Side scraper on a thick blade of Grey Quartzite, upper surface shows median longitudinal high ridge forking at the proximal end slopping on to lateral sides, under surface primary with a prominent bulb of percussion and plain striking platform. The left lateral margin shows steep secondary working to serve for scraping purpose. (82×44×14mm)

2. (YPL) Double sided scraper on thick blade of Grey Quartzite. Upper surface shows a median high longitudinal ridge forking on either end with slopping sides, Under surface primary with a prominent bulb of percussion and a plain striking platform. Both the long lateral margins steeply worked to obtain scraping edges, fresh. (75×43×22mm)

3. (YPL) End scraper on a thin blade-let of Grey Quartzite. Upper surface shows a longitudinal median ridge and another parallel ridge on the right half of the specimen, the distal end shows steep working and both the lateral margin show use marks, fresh. (40×23×9mm)

4. (YPL) Retouched broken blade of Grey Quartzite, upper surface shows two parallel ridges sloppy to the sides. Under surface is primary without bulb. Both the lateral margins thick and minutely retouched, fresh. (29×18×8mm)

5. (YPL) Used broken blade of Grey Quartzite. Upper surface shows two parallel ridges one of the ridges running irregularly. Under surface is primary with a prominent bulb of percussion. The lateral margin shows use marks, fresh. (32×20×9mm)

6. (YPL) Double-sided scraper on a blade-let of Grey Quartzite. Upper surface shows two parallel ridges running wide apart longitudinally with sloppy sides and show deep flake scars. Upper surface is primary with a prominent bulb and bulbar scar. Both the lateral margins are steeply worked to serve scraping, fresh. (56×49×14mm)

CENTRAL BOARD

LETTER 'U'

1. (GPR) Side scraper on a thick end flake of a Chert, the left-hand margin is steeply worked to obtain convex scraping edge. The upper surface shows a longitudinal ridge connected at the centre by horizontal ridge with small shallow and deep flake scars. Under surface is primary with prominent bulb and faceted striking platform, fresh. (40×30×15mm)

2. (GPR) Side scraper on a triangular thick end flake of Chert. Upper surface shows many irregular ridges with shallow and deep flake scars. Under surface is primary with a prominent bulb with prepared striking platform. Both the lateral margins are steeply worked to obtain scraping edges, fresh. (40×35×18mm)

3. (GPR) Round scraper on a thick end flake of Greyish Chert; the scraping edge is obtained all along the periphery by steep flaking; upper surface is fully flaked, under surface is primary with prominent bulb and prepared platform, fresh. (38×30×13mm)

4. (GPR) Round scraper on an end flake of reddish Chert. Scraping edge runs all around the periphery by steep flaking; fresh. (38×33×13mm)

5. (GPR) A retouched flake on an irregular end flake of reddish Chert. Upper surface is fully flaked with shallow flake scars. Under surface is primary with a bulb and striking platform. Secondary working is visible on a part of the periphery; fresh. (38×30×10mm)

6. (GPR) Backed piece on a leaf shaped flaked blade of Chert. Upper surface is fully flaked; Under surface is primary with prominent bulb and prepared striking platform; the right lateral margin is blunted while left lateral margin is tapering right to left minutely retouched to serve cutting purpose; slightly patinated specimen. Patination is clearly seen. (45×34×8mm)

7. (GPR) Backed piece on a flake blade of Agate; upper surface shows a longitudinal median high ridge; Upper surface is primary with a bulb and prepared striking platform. Slightly broken at the distal ends. One of the lateral margins is blunted and the opposite margin shows minute retouch, fresh. (35×24×7mm)

LETTER 'P'

8. (GPR) Retouched blade of dark brown Chert; Upper surface shows a longitudinal median of high ridge; Under surface is primary with a bulb; minute retouch along the right lateral margin and use marks on the left lateral margin, fresh. (35×19×7mm)

9. (GPR) Retouched thick broke blade of Carnelian. Upper surface shows two parallel longitudinal high ridges with a long flake scar in between and tapering on either lateral margin. Under surface is primary with a bulb of percussion; a part of the left lateral margin shows minute retouch towards distal end. The right lateral margin shows used marks, fresh.

10. (GPR) Backed piece on a thick irregular flake of Chert; upper surface is fully flaked with shallow and deep flake scars; under surface is primary with prominent bulb of percussion and a striking platform. Right lateral margin is thick and shows blunting. The left lateral margin is sloppy, comparatively thin and shows retouch for cutting purpose. (52×34×15mm)

11. (GPR) Backed piece on a parallel sided blade of reddish brown Chert; upper surface shows irregular ridges with small shallow and deep scars; Under surface is primary with bulb of percussion; right lateral margin is thick and shows longitudinal flake scar which serves as backing. The left lateral margin is comparatively thin showing minute retouch, fresh. (40×16×9mm)

12. (GPR) Retouched blade of Carnelian broken at distal end; upper side shows two parallel longitudinal ridges in the centre sloping on either margins; under surface is primary with a bulb and prepared striking platform. The left lateral margin shows use marks, while the right lateral margin exhibits minute retouch, fresh. (35×25×10mm)

13. (GPR) A pen-knife blade of Agate; upper surface shows two parallel longitudinal ridges in the centre sloping towards margins on either sides; under surface is primary with diffused bulb of percussion. Right lateral margin is thin exhibiting used marks, the left lateral margin shows discontinuous blunting; fresh. (38×17×6mm)

14. (GPR) Used flakes of ovalish shape; Carnelian; upper surface shows a median ridge joining a horizontal ridge at the distal end; under surface is primary with prominent bulb and facetted striking platform. Use marks are seen all along the periphery, fresh. (40×28×9mm)

15. (GPR) Used flake of irregular Carnelian; upper surface is fully flaked with shallow and deep scars; with sloppy (tapering) margins. Under surface is primary with prominent bulb and prepared striking platform. Use marks are visible on the periphery here and there, fresh. (50×35×10mm)

'Z'-PATTERN

16. (GPR) Macro Lunate on a slender broken blade of fine grained Quartzite; Upper surface shows two parallel ridges running wide apart. Under surface is primary. The arc is carefully blunted. The chord shows minute excellent retouch, fresh. (38×15×5mm)

17. (GPR) Lunate on a broken blade of black banded Agate. Upper surfacc shows irregular ridge with shallow and deep flake scars. Under surface is primary with bulb of percussion. The arc is blunted by bold retouch by margins of alternate flaking. The chord is minutely retouched, fresh. (36×15×8mm)

18. (GPR) Crescent point on a slender blade of Carnelian, the arc is convex and shows excellent step retouched arc at the distal end, dorsal and ventral surfaces are primary, fresh. (48×13×5mm)

19. (GPR) Backed piece on a thick broken blade of Carnelian, dorsal surface with a ridge with a shallow and deep flake scars, ventral surface primary with a bulb of percussion, the left lateral margin shows steep blunting the right lateral margin with use marks, fresh.

20. (GPR) Backed piece on thick blade of Agate, dorsal surface shows a shallow large central flake scar sloping towards right side, the ventral surface is primary with a bulb. The left lateral margin is convex and shows blunting by steep bold flaking, while the right lateral margin had minute retouch, fresh. (46×80×10mm)

21. (GPR) Backed piece on a thick long broken blade of banded Chert. Dorsal surface shows two irregular longitudinal ridges running parallel wide apart. Ventral surface is primary without bulb and platforms. Left lateral margin shows blunting while the right lateral margin shows minute retouch occasionally, fresh.

22. (GPR) Backed piece on a thick blade of Chert. Dorsal surface fully flaked. Ventral surface is primary with a bulb of percussion. Steep flaking blunts the left lateral margin. The right lateral margin is minutely retouched on ventral surface, fresh.

23. (GPR) Backed blade on a Grey Chert. Dorsal surface flaked. Ventral surface is primary with no traces of bulb and platform. The left lateral margin blunted by careful minute retouch. The right lateral margin shows used marks, fresh. (43×17×7mm)

24. (GPR) Backed piece on a thick blade of Chert. Dorsal surface shows a thick high ridge with shallow and deep flake scars. Ventral surface is primary with bulb and bulbar scars. The left lateral margin is thick and blunted while the right lateral margin is thin and shows occasional minute retouch, fresh. (54×23×13mm)

25. (GPR) Backed piece on a thick broken blade of reddish Chert. Dorsal surface shows a high thick ridge forked at the proximal end. Ventral surface is primary with a small bulb and striking platform. The right lateral margin is thick and shows occasional blunting. The left lateral margin shows use marks.

26. (GPR) Thick retouched blade on brownish Agate, dorsal surface shows two high longitudinal parallel ridges wide apart. The left lateral margin is minutely retouched. The right lateral margin shows occasional retouch. Ventral surface is primary with a bulb of percussion and bulbar scar. Striking platform is removed, fresh.

27. (GPR) Retouched blade of Agate. Upper surface shows three ridges running irregular with shallow flake scars. Under surface primary with no bulb and prepared striking platform. Both the lateral margins are minutely retouched, fresh.

28. (GPR) Slightly broken retouched blade of Chalcedony. Upper surface shows a high ridge with shallow and deep flake scars. Under surface is primary with a diffused bulb by the removal of striking platform. One of the margins shows excellent minute retouch. The opposite margin shows use marks, fresh.

29. (GPR) A thick retouched blade core of Carnelian. Upper surface shows two irregular ridges with shallow and deep flake scars, under surface is primary with no traces of bulb or platform. A part of the lateral margin shows retouch. Other margins shows use marks, fresh. (47×14×6mm)

30. (GPR) A thick retouched blade of Agate. Upper surface shows two high ridges with shallow flake scars and a longitudinal patch of cortex on the right half of the blade. Under surface primary with a primary bulb of percussion and a prepared striking platform. Left lateral margin shows excellent minute retouch. Right lateral margin shows use marks. (45×14×8mm)

31. (GPR) Retouched blade of Agate converging towards the distal end. Upper surface shows a high ridge forked at different intervals. Under surface is primary with a prominent bulb of percussion and prepared platform. The lateral margins show occasional retouch and used marks, fresh.

32. (GPR) Retouched blade of Agate. Dorsal surface shows two parallel ridges with shallow and deep flake scars. Under surface is primary with occasional flaking along the margins. One of the margins shows minute retouch. Other margin shows use marks. fresh.

33. (GPR) Retouched blade of Chert, broken at the proximal end. Dorsal surface shows a forked high ridge with sloppy sides. One of the lateral margins is retouched fully. The ventral surface is primary, fresh.

34. (GPR) Retouched blade on a Chert, upper surface shows a median ridge with shallow flake scars, under surface primary with a prominent bulb of percussion, one of the margin shows minute retouch and at the distal end, the opposite margin shows use marks, fresh.

35. (GPR) Retouched blade on banded Chert broken at the distal end, upper surface shows many ridges with shallow and deep flake scars, under surface primary with a prominent bulb, one of margins show minute retouch and opposite margin shows use marks, fresh.

36. (GPR) Burin on a flake blade of Chert, upper surface shows a longitudinal median ridge, under surface primary with no faces of bulb and platform. A vertical burin spall is removed on one of the lateral margins at the proximal end, fresh.

37. (GPR) Burin a thick bladc of Carnelian, upper surface shows many irregular ridges with a shallow and deep flake scars under surface primary with no traces of bulb. Burin edge is obtained at the proximal end by the removal of vertical spall on either side margins, fresh.

38. (GPR) Burin on a thick pointed blade of banded Grey Chert. Upper surface shows a high longitudinal ridge with shallow and deep flake scars, under surface primary with a prominent bulb and bulbar scar, burin edge is created at the proximal end by removal of vertical spall at the proximal end, fresh. (50×20×10mm)

39. (GPR) A blade with used marks of Carnelian; upper surface shows two ridges.

One of the ridges forked at both ends with shallow and deep flake scars. Under surface primary with prominent bulb of percussion and prepared striking platform.

40. (GPR) A broad blade with use marks on either margins of Carnelian, upper surface shows a median of longitudinal ridge with two more ridges on either side wide apart. Under surface primary with a bulb and bulbar scar and plain striking platform, fresh.

41. (GPR) A parallel sided blade, Carnelian, upper surface shows a high median ridge forked on either ends with shallow flake scars, under surface primary with no traces of bulb and platform. Use marks are visible on either longitudinal margin. (46×15×7mm)

42. (GPR) A parallel sided thick blade of Cherty Quartzite, upper surface shows two irregular longitudinal ridges with shallow and deep flake scars, under surface primary with diffused bulb. Use marks are visible on one of the lateral margins, fresh.

43. (GPR) A used blade of Carnelian, upper surface shows a high ridge, forked on either ends with shallow and deep flake scars, under surface primary with a prominent bulb and bulbar scar. Used marks on either lateral margins, fresh.

44. (GPR) A used pointed blade of Carnelian, upper surface shows many longitudinal ridges joining at the distal end with shallow and deep flake scars, under surface primary with a bulb, fresh.

45. (GPR) A used blade on Chalcedony slightly broken at the distal end, upper surface shows two longitudinal ridges with shallow flake scars. Under surface primary with a prominent bulb of percussion, fresh.

46. (GPR) A used blade of Chert, upper surface shows two irregular ridges with small deep flake scars. Under surface is primary with a bulb, fresh.

47. (GPR) A blade converging into a point at the distal end on reddish Chert, upper surface primary with a bulb. Use marks are visible on either side margin, fresh.

48. (GPR) A thick fresh rejuvenated irregular core of Cherty Quartzite, upper surface shows a high ridge with shallow and deep flake scars and a patch of cortex, under surface primary with a tale of bulb. One of the margins is straight and parallel and the opposite margins convex or irregular. The lateral margins show occasional retouch, fresh.

49. (GPR) A retouched flake blade on Carnelian, upper surface shows a median ridge with small shallow and deep flake scars with occasional patches or cortex. Under surface is primary with a bulb and bulbar scar. Minute retouch on either lateral margins and at the distal end, fresh. (Not Illustrated)

50. (GPR) A thick flake blade of Carnelian with irregular margins slightly broken

at the distal end, upper surface shows, two longitudinal ridges running irregularly with shallow and deep flake scars. Under surface primary with bulb and prepared striking platform, bulb is removed. Careful retouch is noticed all along the periphery, fresh. (Not Illustrated)

51. (GPR) A broken retouched blade of Chert, upper surface shows longitudinal ridges with shallow flake scars, Under surface shows shallow and deep flake scars, leaving a patch of primary surface. Both the lateral margins are minutely worked to obtain sharp cutting edges, fresh. (Not Illustrated)

52. (GPR) A thick blade of Cherty Quartzite. Upper surface shows many longitudinal ridges extending from the proximal end to the distal end with shallow and deep flake scars, under surface primary with a bulb and bulbar scar and plain striking platform, one of the long lateral margins shows minute retouch, fresh.

53. (GPR) A thick pointed flake blade of Cherty Quartzite. Upper surface shows a longitudinal ridge, forked at the distal end, with long shallow and small deep flake scars, under surface primary with prominent bulb and bulbar scar and peripheral striking platform. One of the lateral margins shows excellent retouch and its opposite margin shows use marks, fresh.

54,55. (GPR) A small thick retouched blade with a straight convex margin, on dark brown Chert, upper surface – along median ridge forked on either ends, under surface primary with a bulbar scar, the straight margin shows retouch, fresh.

FIRST ROW

56. (GPR) Side scraper on an irregular flake of Chert; Upper surface shows an irregular ridge with shallow and deep scars; under surface partially flaked with no trace of bulb. One of the lateral margins has steep working to obtain scraping edge, fresh.

57. (GPR) Side scraper on a thick flake of Cherty Quartzite; Upper surface shows forked ridge with shallow and deep flake scars; under surface is primary with no trace of bulb. One of the lateral margins is thick with minute retouch. The lateral margins is thin showing steep flaking to serve as scraping edge, fresh. (48×17×15mm)

58. (GPR) Double scraper on a flake blade of Cherty Quartzite; upper surface shows a long deep and many shallow flake scars. Under surface is partly flaked with a prominent bulb of percussion and prepared striking platform. Both the long lateral margins are steeply worked to serve scraping, fresh.

59. (GPR) End scraper on a thick blade of Agate; upper surface shows high ridges running parallel with shallow and deep scars; Under surface primary with no traces of bulb and striking platform. The broad distal end exhibits steep minute flaking, fresh.

60. (GPR) End scraper on a small flake blade of Carnelian; upper surface shows a

median ridge flaked at the proximal end. The distal end is steeply worked to obtain scraping edge; under surface is primary with diffused bulb and prepared striking platform, fresh.

61. (GPR) End scraper on a narrow flake of Chert; upper surface is flaked; under surface is primary; one of the ends is convex and shows steep secondary work to serve scraping, fresh. (54×20×8mm)

SECOND ROW

62. (GPR) Double sided scraper on a thick flake blade of Chert broken at the distal end; upper surface shows irregular discontinuous ridges with small shallow and deep flake scars. Under surface primary with a bulb of percussion with bulbar scar and faceted striking platform. Both the long lateral margins by steep retouch to serve as scraping edge, fresh. (56×30×12mm)

63. (GPR) Double edged side cum end scraper on a thick blade on a banded elert, upper surface shows two parallel ridges running irregularly length wise joining at the bulbar scar both the lateral margins and the proximal end are steeply flaked to obtain scraping edges, fresh.

64. (GPR) Side cum end scraper on a flake of Chert; upper surface shows shallow and deep flake scars with a patch of cortex, under surface primary with prominent bulb and bulbar scars and prepared striking platform. Steep flaking is noticeable all along the periphery to serve scraping, fresh.

65. (GPR) Side cum end scraper on a flake of Chert, upper surface shows a median longitudinal ridge forking at the distal end, under surface primary with a prominent bulb and striking platform. Steep flaking observed all along the periphery, fresh.

66. (GPR) Side cum end scraper on a blade of Chert, upper surface shows many irregular ridges with shallow and deep flake scars, under surface primary with bulb and bulbar scar and a striking platform. Steep minute flaking noticed all along the periphery, fresh. (45×22×9mm)

67. (GPR) Round scraper on a triangular flake of Chalcedony upper surface fully flaked with small shallow flake scars, under surface primary with bulbar scar with prepared striking platform, steep flaking all along the periphery to obtain scarping edge, fresh.

67a. (GPR) Round scraper on an ovalish flake of Carnelian, upper surface shows many shallow flake scars, under surface primary with a prominent bulb and bulbar scar. Scraping edge is obtained all along the periphery by steep flaking, fresh. (31×27×11mm) (Not Illustrated)

67b. (GPR) Round scraper on a squarish flake of Cherty Quartzite, upper surface shows small shallow and deep flake scars with many ridges, under surface primary with no traces of bulb and striking platform. Scraping edge is created all along the periphery by steep flaking, fresh. (Not Illustrated)

THIRD ROW

68. (GPR) Notched scrapers on a Lunate shaped thick flake of Chert, upper surface fully flaked with shallow and deep flake scars, under surface partly flaked with bulbar scars, one of the long lateral margins a notch is created by removal of a session of flaking, fresh.

69. (GPR) Side cum hollow scraper on a triangular flake on Cherty Quartzite, both the surfaces are fully flaked; one of the margins a hollow is created by removal of one large flake followed by minute secondary working, the other two margins are steeply flaked to obtain scraping edges, fresh.

70. (GPR) Core scraper on a small core of Agate, steep flaking all along the periphery to obtain scraping edge, fresh.

71. (GPR) Scraper on a small plano-convex pebble reddish Chert, steep flaking is noticed all along the periphery, fresh. (37×23×17mm)

72. (GPR) Thick used flake blade of Carnelian. Both the margins converge into a point at the distal end and shows use marks, upper surface shows a high longitudinal median ridge forked at the proximal end and sloping margins, under surface primary with a bulb with no traces of platform, fresh.

73. (GPR) Parallel side used blade of Agate upper surface shows a longitudinal median ridge with a prominent bulb and prepared striking platform occasional use marks on both the margins, fresh.

FOURTH ROW

74. (GPR) Parallel sided blade of Quartzite, one lateral margin straight and the opposite margin is converging to a point, upper surface shows longitudinal ridges with long shallow and small deep flake scars, under surface primary with a prominent bulb of percussion and a plain striking platform, fresh.

75. (GPR) Parallel sided blade of Quartzite, upper surface partly flaked and partly retains cortex, under surface primary with a prominent bulb of percussion, with prepared platform, use marks on both the margins, fresh.

76. (GPR) Used blade of Carnelian converging into a point at the distal end, upper surface shows two parallel-sided ridges with shallow and deep flake scars under surface primary with a bulb and bulbar scar and a plain striking platform, fresh.

77. (GPR) Borer cum scraper on a flake of Chalcedony, upper surface shows many small shallow and deep flake scars, under surface partly flaked with a prominent bulb of percussion, both the margins are steeply flaked with a prominent bulb of percussion.

The margins are steeply flaked to obtain scraping edge, borer point is obtained at the distal end, and borer tip is prepared by careful secondary working on either sides of the tip, fresh.

78. (GPR) Scraper- cum -borer on an irregular flake of Chert. One of the margins steeply flaked on either surfaces which is convex, the opposite margin is flaked from under surface, borer point is obtained at the distal end by careful trimming on either margins, fresh.

79. (GPR) Borer cum scraper on a small-elongated core of Chert, one of the margins are steeply flaked from either surface, its opposite margin is pointed and made as borer tip by careful secondary working on either side, fresh. (45×27×15mm)

FIFTH ROW

80. (GPR) A thick blade of reddish Chert. Upper surface shows two longitudinal irregular ridges with shallow and deep flake scars. Under surface primary with a bulb and bulbar scar, proximal end is thinned by removal of small deep flake scars on the upper surface, a part of the periphery shows minute retouch and a part of it is with use marks, fresh.

81. (GPR) A small broad used blade of Chalcedony, upper surface a forked ridge with a small patch of cortex and shallow and deep flake scars, under surface primary with a prominent bulb of percussion and prepared striking platform, fresh.

82. (GPR) A used broad blade of Agate, upper surface a longitudinal ridge with a patch of cortex at the distal end, under surface primary with a prominent bulb of percussion and prepared striking platform, fresh.

83. (GPR) A small thick broad used blade of Carnelian. Upper surface shows a longitudinal median ridge with shallow and deep flake scars. Under surface is primary with a prominent bulb and bulbar scar and facetted striking platform, fresh. (33×20×9mm)

84. (GPR) An irregular flake of Chert Quartzite, upper surface shows small shallow and deep flake scars with a patch of cortex. Under surface is primary with a prominent bulb of percussion and a facetted striking platform. Both the lateral margins and at the distal end, careful and minute retouch is noticeable, fresh. (43×29×13mm)

85. (GPR) Retouched pointed flake of reddish Chalcedony, upper surface shows shallow and deep flake scars, under surface primary with a prominent bulb of percussion and facetted striking platform. Both the lateral margins are minutely retouched, fresh. (42×38×11mm)

SIXTH ROW

86. (GPR) A conical fluted core of reddish Chert with a broad platform and parallel sided and irregular flutings on its body, fresh. (43×48×38mm)

87. (GPR) A conical flake core of brown Chert with a flat platform on one end and the other converges to a conical form. Irregular squarish and ovalish flake scars are prominent all along the body with a patch of cortex here and there, fresh. (52×64×41mm)

88. (GPR) A conical fluted core of Grey Carnelian. Parallel wide flutings are visible on its body. (50×31×24mm)

89. (GPR) A blade of Grey Chert parallel flutings are present on the dorsal side. (48×31×22mm)

90. (GPR) A thick broken blade of Reddish Chert with flutings on dorsal side. (48×31×20mm)

91. (GPR) A thick flake of Reddish Chalcedony with a Cortex. (38×34×20mm)

92. (GPR) A thick flake of Carnelian with retouch on the right lateral margin. (35×25×20mm)

REFERENCES

Flinte, R. F. 1963 Pleistocene Climates in Low Altitude, *Geographical Review,* 53-1.

Foote, R. B. *Prehistoric and Protohistoric Antiquities Of India.*

Ghosh, A. 1948 Prehistoric Explorations in India, IHC 24.

Ghosh, A. K. 1961 Prehistoric Studies in Eastern India, SC. Cul 27.

Sen, D. & Ghosh, A. D. (Eds.) 1966 Implements from Late Site in Eastern India in Studies in Prehistory B. R. Foote Memorial Volume, Calcutta.

- 1970 *The Palaeolithic Culture of Singhbhum,* Transection of the American Philosophical Society

Hegde, K. Tm. M. 1972 Physics and Chemistry in Indian *Archaeology, Archaeological Congress* and Seminar Papers (Ed. S. B. Deo) Nagpur, pp. 133-141.

Joshi, R. V. & Khare, M. D. 1966 Microlithic bearing deposits of Adamgarh Rock Shelters in *Studies in Prehistory* Eds. D. Sen and A. K. Ghosh, Calcutta, 90-95.

Joshi & *Bopardikar, B. P.* 1972 Stone age cultures of Konkan in *Archaeological Congress and Seminar Papers* Ed. S. B. Deo, Nagpur 47-51.

1973 *The Significance of Microlithic Tools in Post Palaeolithic Industries.*

Khan, E. 1968 Pleistocene Stratigraphy in India. *Annals of the Geology Department,* Vol. IV, Alligrah.

Joshi, R. V. 1978 *Stone age cultures of Central India,* Deccan College, Post Graduate and Research Institute, Poona.

1979 Bhokar – A Upper Palaeolithic Factory Site from Central Godavary Basin, Maharashtra, *Man and Environment, III.*

Chittale, Rajaguru, S.V., Pappu, S. N. & Badam, R. S. 1981 Archaeological Studies in the Manjra Valley, Central Godavary Basin, *Bulletin of Deccan College,* Research Institute.

Srinivasan, L. K. 1960-61 Indian Archaeology—A review.

Lal, B. B. 1958 Birbhampoor, A Microlithic Site in the Damodar Valley, West Bengal, AI – Vol. 4

Murthy, M. L. K. 1966 *The Stone Age Cultures of Chittor District,* Ph. D. Unpublished thesis, Poona University.

1968 Blade and Burin Industries Near Reniguntaon South east Coast of India, *Proceedings of Prehistoric Society* (N. S.) XXXIV 83-101.

1970 Blade and Burin and Late Stone Age Industries, around Renigunta, Chitoor District, I.A.4.

1974 A Late Pleistocene Cave Site In Southern Indian PA. Ps.

Murthy, M. L. K 1974 Late Pleistocene Fauna and Kurnool Caves, South India, in A.T. Clason (Ed.) *Archaeological Studies* (Amastardam)

Timma Reddy, K. 1976 The significance of lithic Finds in Cave Areas of Kurnool *Asian Perspectives* 18.

Murthy, M. L. K. 1979 Recent Research in the Upper Palaeolithic Phase in India, *Journal of Field Archaeology.*

Chapter —VI

Mesolithic Period (20,000–5,000 B. P.)

The term Mesolithic has been variously described in Indian context as Epi-Palaeolithic, Proto-Neolithic and Late Stone Age. Allchins (1968) observe that Microliths occur in sub-soil contexts. These are spread through out the country and occur in varied geomorphic situations. Mishra (1967) classified the Mesolithic sites as littoral, reverine, rock-shelter and open air sites. The available carbon 14 determinations indicate that the Mesolithic Phase began some 10000 years ago and continued till the onset of the Neolithic, some 4,500 years ago. Microliths form part of the Neolithic ensemble and in certain areas they were in use even in early historic times (Subba Rao, personality of India). Through this long period of time in which the microliths were used, the Mesolithic societies under went changes. Some of the changes may be accounted for cultural influences from outside culture areas. It is in this way that the Mesolithic folk acquired pottery and Metallurgy. Lal (1958 A14) try to interpret the Mesolithic evidences in this country under separate heads, Aceramic-Mesolithic and Ceramic-Mesolithic and non-geometric and geometric-Mesolithic industries. Birbhanpoor (1958), Sanganakallu (Foote 1916; Subba Rao 1948), Terisites (1956), Sarai Naharrai are among the important examples of Aceramic and non-geometric Microlithic industries. Langhnaj (Sankalia 1956) and Bagor are among the best known examples for ceramic Geometric and Microlithic industries. This classification of the Microlithic industry in India has the stratigraphic conformation from Belan Valley and Lekhania (1930,1961-63).

Todd (1950), discovered around Bombay several Mesolithic sites on rock out crops. The industry composed of blades, backed pieces, triangles, trapezes, scrapers, mace heads etc., and shows advanced nature. Sali (1980) at Patne found Microlithic culture in a three-meter thick deposit. And, the industry comprising both geometric and crested ridge blades. Zeuner and Allchin (1956) in Tamilnadu found several Teresites.

The industry comprises backed and obliquely blunted blades scrapers, points, lunates, triangles, chopping tools and discoids. These sites are dated to about 4,000 B.C., Paddaiah (1968-70, 1971,1972,1974) discovered over 30 Microlithic sites in Shorapur, Karnataka, and the industry is Non-Geometric in nature.

A number of Microlithic bearing localities were discovered in different parts of A.P.. Foote (1916), Cammiade (1924), Cammiade and Burkit (1930), Soundar Rajan (1958), Isaac (1960), Nagabhushana Rao (1966), Krishna Murthy (1970), Kasturi Bai

(1982) and Sastry D. L. N. (1984). Significant among these discoverics were Cammiade's in the lower Godavari Valley and pointed out Microlithic occurrences at more than hundred sites. At Nagarjunakonda microliths occurred in two feet thick gravel wash, and the assemblage is non-geometric and aceramic. In Kurnool and Prakasam Districts of Andhra Pradesh, microliths occur on surface. The assemblage consists of scrapers, borers, burins, blades and backed pieces. In the lime stone areas of Kurnool district Murty and Timma Reddy discovered several microlithic sites, and they are aceramic and non-geometric. Rami Reddy (1975) discovered 14 microlithic sites in Kurnool and Ananthapur districts, and they are Non-Geometric and Aceramic. S. N. Rao (1966) discovered several microlithic factory sites and the industry is Non-Geometric and Aceramic. D. L. N. Sastry discovered 33 Microlithic localities in Medak district and they are Non-Geometric and aceramic, and the culture may be datable to the time bracket 9,000–4,000 B.C.

Plate XV

Principle, Lower, Middle, Upper and Microlithic Sites in India and in Andhra Pradesh

Plate XVI

Tool Types of the Mesolithic Period—A Transitory Period Between Food Gathering and Food Producing

TOOLS FOUND AT SITES IN ANDHRA PRADESH	
Board I (1-34)	123 to 127. Side Scrapers
1 to 7. Cores	Board IV (128-146)
8 to19. End Flakes	128 to 130. Double Sided Scrapers
20 to 34. Fluted Cores	131 to 134. End Scrapers
Board II (35-74)	135 to 141. Side Scrapers
35 to 50. Parallel Sided Blades	142. Round scraper
51. Irregular Blade	143. Crescent shaped flake
52 to 58. Thick Blades	144. Irregular flake
59. Retouched Blade	145. Oval flake
60 to 74. Thick blades	146. Triangular flake
Board III (75-127)	Board V (147-169)
75 to 114. Baked blades	147 to 149. Hollow Scrapers
115,116. Parallel sided blades	150. Double hollow scraper
117. Broad blade	151 to 154. Side-Cum-Hollow End Scraper
118 to 122. Pen Knife Blades	155,156. Hollow Scrapers

157 to 165. Scrapers 166 to 167. Borer Cum Scraper 168. Blade 169. Flake Board VI (170-185) 170 to 181 Crescent Point 182 to 185 Burins	Board VII (186-199) 186 to 192 Lunates 193 to 198 Triangles 199 Trapeze

DESCRIPTION OF MESOLITHIC TOOLS

BOARD I

1. Ovalish flake core of Cherty pebble, irregular flake scars are visible on either surfaces, patina on under surface, fresh. (35×37.3×20mm)

2. Ovalish flake scar of Chalcedony, rectangular ovalish and irregular flake scars on either surfaces, large part of one of the surface is covered by cortex except for the presence of few flakes, fresh. (37.4×34.5×16.5mm)

3. Roughly cylindrical flake of brown chert, leaving patches of cortex here and there. Flake scars all over the body are visible; flakes are removed multi directionally, fresh. (35×23.3×22.8mm)

4. Roughly cylindrical amorphous pebble core of Chalcedony, ovalish, rectangular and irregular flake scars are noticed all around the body with a patch of cortex, fresh. (29.6×21.3×18.5mm)

5. An irregular shaped amorphous core of jasper, ovalish and irregular shaped flakes or removed in multi directions, fresh. (33×26.5×16.5mm)

6. Irregular shaped amorphous core of Chalcedony; a few ovalish and irregular flake scars are visible, fresh. (26.3×23.5×17.5mm)

7. Irregular shaped core of Chalcedony, a few ovalish and irregular flake scars are visible on the body of the core with occasional patches of cortex, fresh. (29.3×25.5×15mm)

8. Roughly triangular end flake of Carnelian upper surface shows a forked ridge and small shallow and deep flake scars especially at the posterior end, under surface shows primary flake scars with a prominent bulb of percussion. Minute retouch on both the lateral margins, fresh. (23×12.5×5mm)

9. Irregular end flake of Carnelian, a forked ridge with shallow and deep fake scars on the upper surface with a cortical patch along the right lateral margin, bulb of percussion and ripple marks on the under surface, use marks on the upper half of the left lateral margin, fresh.(28×14×3.5mm)

10. Irregular shaped end flake of Carnelian upper surface shows a forked ridge, forked, under surface primary with a prominent bulb of percussion and a prepared striking platform, minute retouch on left lateral margin, fresh. (23.5×17.5×4mm)

11. Thin flake of Carnelian, two narrow parallel ridges at the middle with shallow and deep flake scars on either side of the upper surface, primary f lake surface on the under surface, occasional use marks on the right lateral margin, fresh. (24×12×4mm)

12. Elongated oval end flake of Chalcedony, upper surface shows deep and shallow flake scars with irregular ridges, under surface shows a bulb of percussion and ripple marks throughout the surface, occasional use marks along the margin, fresh. (27.2×15×3.5mm)

13. Thin irregular side flake of Chalcedony with shallow and deep flake scars on the upper surface. Prominent bulb of percussion and primary flake surface with the removal of few flakes along left margin on the under surface and prepared platform, use marks on a part of the right lateral margin, fresh. (31.4×17.5×3mm)

14. A pointed end flake of Chalcedony with a median longitudinal ridge on the dorsal surface, primary flake surface with a very prominent bulb of percussion on the ventral surface and a facetted platform, use marks all along the periphery, fresh. (20×13.5×4.3mm)

15. A thin pointed end Grey flake of chert. Dorsal surface shows two parallel ridges on the left half of the flake with long and shallow deep flake scars, ventral surface shows primary flake surface and a bulb of percussion. Occasional use marks on the left lateral margin minute retouch on the right lateral margin, fresh. (27.5×14.5×2.5mm)

16. An irregular end flake of chert, dorsal surface shows irregular ridges with shallow and deep flake scars, ventral surface shows primary flake surface with traces of bulb, occasional use-marks on the right lateral margin, fresh. (31×16.5×5.8mm)

17. An irregular end flake, shallow and deep flake scar on the upper surface, primary flake surface with traces of bulb on the lower surface, thick diffuse end and thin proximal end use-marks on the right lateral margin, fresh. (26×12.5×6.8mm)

18. A roughly rectangular end flake of Carnelian converging into a point. Dorsal surface shows an irregular ridge with large shallow and deep small flake scars, under surface shows primary flake surface with no traces of bulb and a prepared platform, use-marks all around the lateral margins, fresh. (27×13.5×4.5mm)

19. An irregular thick end flake of Chalcedony, upper surface shows two median parallel ridges with shallow and deep flake scars under surface shows la primary flake surface with bulbar scar, use-marks all along the periphery, fresh. (21×13×4.8mm)

20. Roughly conical fluted core pebble of brown chert, parallel-sided flutations on part of its body, fresh. (37.5×31×18mm)

21. Fragment of roughly cylindrical fluted core of Agate, parallel-sided flutations around its body with a patch of cortex, fresh. (35×25×12mm)

22. Fragment of conical fluted core of chert, with parallel-sided flutation on part of its body and the other end convergent into conical form, fresh. (42×26×14mm)

23. Cylindrical fluted core Chalcedony; parallel side flutations are on part of its body with a striking flat platform on one end, fresh. (30.5×27×19.5mm)

24. Conical fluted core of jasper one end shows a flat striking platform and the other end converging into a blunt point, rectangular ovalish and irregular flake scars found all along its body, fresh. (30×26×19mm)

25. Roughly cylindrical fluted core of Chalcedony with parallel side flutations part of its body, fresh. (37.5×23.5×15mm)

26. Cylindrical fluted core of Grey Chert, flake scars are removed all along its body in two directions, fresh. (38×22×15mm)

27. Cylindrical fluted core of Agate, a flat striking platform is noticed on one end, with parallel side flutation around a part of its body, fresh. (25×23×20mm)

28. Conical fluted core of chert, parallel side flutations all around its body removed in two directions with a patch of cortex towards pointed end, fresh. (35×20×18mm)

29. A cylindrical residual fluted core of Chalcedony, excellent parallel side flutations on part of its body with prepared striking platform on one end, fresh. (40×20×10mm)

30. Roughly shaped conical fluted core of Agate with a two flat striking platforms, parallel sided flutations and ovalish flake scars all along its body, oriented in two directions, fresh. (30×27×25mm)

31. Fragment of a cylindrical core of Chalcedony with rectangular and irregular flutations around part of its body with a patch of cortex, fresh. (34×22×14.5mm)

32. Conical fluted core of brown Chert with striking platform at one end, pointed other end, parallel side flutations around a part of its body with a patch of cortex, fresh. (31×21×20mm)

33. Conical fluted core of Carnelian, striking platform on one end and pointed on the other end, parallel sided flutations around part of its body, fresh. (30×24.5×18mm)

34. Roughly cylindrical residual fluted core of jasper, parallel side flutations and ovalish flake scars all along the body in two directions, fresh. (32×15×14.5mm)

BOARD II

35. Parallel side thick blade of Agate with a pointed distal end. Dorsal surface shows three parallel-sided ridges with shallow and deep longitudinal flake scars. Under surface primary with a prominent bulb of percussion, fresh. (49×13×6.2mm)

36. Blade of Chert. Dorsal surface shows two longitudinal parallel ridges with large shallow and deep flake scars. Under surface primary with a prominent bulb, fresh. (44.5×11.5×4.2mm)

37. Parallel sided blade on banded Agate. Upper surface shows a median ridge forked at one end with shallow and deep small flake scars. Under surface primary with no traces of bulb, fresh. (36×12.5×3mm)

38. A small parallel sided blade of Grey Chert. Upper surface shows a forked median ridge with shallow and deep flake scars. Under surface primary with a prominent bulb of percussion, fresh. (23×6.5×2.5mm)

39. Parallel sided thin blade of Carnelian. Upper surface shows two longitudinal parallel-sided ridges. Under surface primary with no traces of bulb, fresh. (31.3×7.3×2mm)

40. Thick blade of Agate. Upper surface shows a high median ridge. Bulb of percussion is present near the distal end. Minute flakes are removed on the dorsal surface perhaps to reduce the thickness of the blade. Use marks are on both the margins, fresh. (52.5×11.3×6.4mm)

41. A thick pointed blade on Cherty Carnelian. Upper surface shows a central high ride forked at the proximal end. Under surface is primary with a prominent bulb, fresh. (42.2×13.8×6.7mm)

42. Broad parallel sided blade of Carnelian. Upper surface shows two parallel sided longitudinal rides running wide a part. Under surface primary with ripple marks, fresh. (41.1×18.1×3.5mm)

43. A thick blade with straight and convex margins of Carnelian upper surface shows a high central ridge forked on either end. Upper surface is primary with a prominent bulb of percussion. Left lateral margin shows retouch and a part of right lateral margin with use marks, fresh. (37.3×12.5×5.7mm)

44. Thick blade of Chalcedony, it narrows at the proximal end and broad at the distal end. Perhaps broken. Upper surface shows shallow and deep longitudinal flake scars forming irregular ridges. Under surface is primary with a bulb of percussion. Occasional use marks on both the margins, fresh. (38.5×13.4×5 mm)

45. Thick parallel sided blade on banded Agate. Upper surface shows a median

high ridge forked from the middle. Under surface primary with a bulb. Use marks are on either margins, fresh. (36.3×9.5×5mm)

46. Parallel sided blade of Chalcedony. A longitudinal high ridge on the dorsal surface, a prominent bulb of percussion on the ventral surface. Use marks are on either margins, fresh. (30×13.2×32mm)

47. Slightly broken blade on brown Chert. A median high forked ridge on the dorsal surface. Primary flake surface with a bulb of percussion on the ventral surface. Use marks are on either margins, fresh. (27.3×7.5×3.2mm)

48. Parallel sided blade of Chert. Two parallel ridges with large shallow and small, shallow and deep flake scars on either half. Primary flake surface with a bulbar scar on the ventral surface. One margin shows fine minute retouch and the opposite margin with use marks, fresh. (31.5×9.5×3.8mm)

49. A thick blade of Carnelian. Upper surface shows forked high median ridge with shallow and deep flake scars and two cortical patches. Under surface is with a prominent bulb of percussion and ripple marks. Occasional use marks are on one of the margins, fresh. (38.2×12.5×4.3mm)

50. A parallel sided blade of Chalcedony. Two parallel ridges on the dorsal surface. Ripple marks and a prominent bulb of percussion on the ventral surface. Occasional use marks on either margin, fresh. (42.7×11.3×3mm)

51. Slightly irregular blade of Carnelian. Distal end is comparatively broad and thick and proximal end is converging. Two median closely running parallel ridges on the dorsal surface. A minute bulb and ripple marks on the ventral surface. Use-marks on both the lateral margins, fresh. (50.2×15.7×7.3mm)

52. Thick blade of Chert. Dorsal surface shows a forked ridge. Ventral surface shows primary flake surface with a prominent bulb of percussion and a bulbar scar. Occasional use-marks on either margin, slightly broken at the distal end, fresh. (38.3×15.2×4.5mm)

53. Thick blade of Carnelian, thick at the distal end and right half. Dorsal surface is thick and cortex is present on the ventral surface. Left half is flaked fully. Use-marks are on left lateral margins, fresh. (31.4×11.8×5.1mm)

54. Thick blade of cherty Carnelian, dorsal surface shows a median ridge forked on either side. Ventral surface is primary. Flake surface is with ripple marks slightly broken. Use marks are on one of the margins, fresh. (33.6×13×4.8mm)

55. A blade of Chalcedony. A high median ridge on the upper surface. Under surface is primary, slightly broken at the distal end. Use marks are on either margin, fresh. (22.3×10.5×4mm)

56. Thick blade of cherty Carnelian. Dorsal surface shows a high ridge, forked on either ends. Ventral surface is primary with bulbar scar. Occasional use marks on either margin, fresh. (34×11.2×6.2mm)

57. Thick blade of Carnelian. A high median ridge with small deep, flake scars at the distal end and on the right half of the dorsal surface. Left half of the same surface is with cortex. A prominent bulb of percussion and primary flake surface on the ventral surface. Use marks on both the lateral margins, fresh. (31.1×14.8×6mm)

58. A thick blade of Carnelian. A median high ridge on the dorsal surface. A prominent bulb of percussion with a bulbar scar and primary flake surface on the ventral surface. A part of the left lateral margin minutely worked and with occasional use marks on the right margins, fresh. (41.5×15×8.6mm)

59. Retouched blade of Chalcedony. Dorsal surface shows a ridge with shallow and deep small flake scars and patches. On the left half ventral surface with ripple marks and diffused bulb of percussion. One of the lateral margins is carefully retouched, fresh. (31.4×16×3.5mm)

60. A blade of Chert. Dorsal surface shows three parallel-sided ridges. Ventral surface shows bulbar scar and ripple marks and prepared striking platform. Broken at the distal end one of the lateral margins is minutely retouched and the other margin with use marks, fresh. (26.6×11.7×4.4mm)

61. Thin blade of Carnelian. Dorsal surface shows a median ridge. Ventral surface shows ripple marks and prepared striking platform. One of the margins is minutely retouched and the other margin is with use marks, fresh. (21×8.2×2.3mm)

62. A narrow blade of Carnelian. Dorsal surface shows a median ridge forked. Ventral surface shows primary flake surface and a prepared striking platform. Both the margins show minute retouch, fresh. (22×6.4×3.4mm)

63. A thin and narrow blade of Carnelian. A longitudinal ridge on the dorsal surface. Ripple marks on the ventral surface. Slightly broken at the proximal end. One of the margins is carefully retouched. Other margin shows the used marks, fresh. (22.6×7×2mm)

64. A thick blade of Carnelian. Upper surface shows a high median ridge with a small deep flake scar near the distal end. Lower surface shows primary flake surface with no traces of bulb. One of the margins shows fine secondary working. Other margin with used marks. Broken at the distal end, fresh. (24×10×5mm)

65. A broken thick blade of Chalcedony. Dorsal surface shows a median high ridge forked at the proximal end. Ventral surface shows primary flake surface with a bulbar

scar. Distal end broken. One of the lateral margins is retouched and the other shows used marks, fresh. (3.5×11.2×5mm)

66. A broken thick blade of Chalcedony. Upper surface shows forked high ridge with shallow and deep small scars on either side. Under surface shows primary. Flake surface with a bulb of percussion. Distal end broken. One of the lateral margins is partly retouched, fresh. (29.2×11.3×5mm)

67. A broken broad and thick blade of Chalcedony. Dorsal surface shows a forked ridge with deep and shallow flake scars. Ventral surface shows traces of a bulb and primary flake surface. Both the lateral margins are retouched, fresh. (22×13.8×5mm)

68. A broken thick blade of Carnelian. Dorsal surface shows two irregularly running ridges with deep shallow flake scars. Ventral surface shows primary. Flake surface with a small bulb and bulbar scar. Broken at the distal end. Both the margins are retouched, fresh. (20×13×6.2mm)

69. A thick broke blade of Chalcedony. Dorsal surface shows two parallel ridges. Ventral surface shows primary flake surface with a bulb of percussion. Broken at the distal end. Both the margin shows retouch, fresh. (19.4×9×3mm)

70. A broken blade of Chert. Upper surface shows a median forked ridge. Lower surface shows primary. Flake surface broken on either end. One of the lateral margins shows retouch while the other use-marks, fresh. (18×9×3.5mm)

71. A thin broke blade of Chalcedony. Dorsal surface shows two parallel ridges with very small shallow and deep flake scars in between the ridges. Ventral surface is primary with the bulb of percussion. Both the lateral margins show secondary working, fresh. (17×11×2mm)

72. A thin broken blade of Carnelian. Dorsal surface shows a median high ridge. Ventral surface shows primary flake surface. Broken at the proximal end. Both the margins show minute retouch, fresh. (18×8×3mm)

73. A broken blade of Carnelian. Upper surface shows a median ridge with deep and shallow flakes. Lower surface shows primary flake scars. Both the lateral margins are retouched. Broken at the distal end, fresh. (20×10×4mm)

74. A thin blade of Chalcedony. Broken at the distal end. Dorsal surface shows two parallel ridges. Ventral surface shows primary. Primary flake surface with a bulb. One of the lateral margins is retouched. The other margin shows use-marks, fresh. (20×11×3mm)

BOARD III

75. Backed piece on a blade of Chalcedony. Dorsal surface shows a high ridge on the left half of the blade and forked towards the proximal end. Ventral surface shows a

prominent bulb of percussion and ripple marks. The left lateral margin is thick and serves as natural backing. The right lateral margin is thin and shows excellent retouch, fresh. (41×11.5×4.5mm)

76. Backed piece on a thick blade of Chert. Broken at the distal end. Upper surface shows two longitudinal parallel ridges. Lower surface primary with traces of bulb and prepared striking platform. The left lateral margin is thick and obtained by removal of longitudinal flake. The opposite margin is thin and shows minute retouch to serve cuttings, fresh. (36.8×12.5×4.3mm)

77. Backed piece of Carnelian. Upper surface shows a forked high ridge towards left half of the blade end. The shallow and deep small flake scars on the right half. Under surface is primary with a prominent bulb of percussion. The left lateral margin is thick and serves as backing. While the right lateral margin is thin and sharp and shows use marks, fresh. (34.6×10×4mm)

78. Broken backed piece of Carnelian. Dorsal surface shows a mid ridge. Ventral surface shows a diffused bulb of percussion and ripple marks. Left lateral margin is thick and serves as natural backing while the right lateral margin is thin and sharp and shows use marks, fresh. (31.4×10×3mm)

79. A thick backed piece of Agate. Dorsal surface shows longitudinal ridge on the left half and a patch of cortex on the right half. Ventral surface shows primary flake surface with diffused bulb of percussion. The right lateral margin is thick with cortex serving as natural backing. The left lateral margin shows use-marks, fresh. (28.7×11.5×5mm)

80. Thick backed piece at Chert. A high forked ridge on the right half of a longitudinal ridge with thin edge on left half of the dorsal surface. Primary flake surface with a prominent bulb of percussion on the ventral surface. The right lateral margin is thick and serves for backing. The left lateral margin is with use-marks, fresh. (31×11.5×6mm)

81. Thick backed piece of Chalcedony. Dorsal surface mostly flaked and shows shallow and deep small flake scars leaving a longitudinal patch of cortex on the left margin. Ventral surface shows a prominent bulb of percussion and main flake surface. The right lateral margin is thick with natural surface serving as backing and the left lateral margin shows occasional use-marks, fresh. (34.3×11×4mm)

82. Backed piece on thick parallel-sided flake of Carnelian. Dorsal surface is fully flaked with shallow and deep long flake scars. Ventral surface is primary, flake surface with a bulb part removed. Right lateral margin is thick with the removal of a few flakes serving as backing. The left lateral margin comparatively thin and occasional use-marks, fresh. (37.5×10.4×5.5mm)

83. Backed piece of Agate. Dorsal surface shows two parallel longitudinal ridges. Ventral surface is primary. Flake surface is with a bulb of percussion. The left lateral margin is thick with a patch of cortex serving as natural backing, while the right lateral margin is thin with use-marks, fresh. (25×10.5×3mm)

84. A broken backed piece on Chalcedony. Dorsal surface shows two longitudinal closely running parallel ridges with deep and shallow flake scars in between. The ventral surface shows a prominent bulb of percussion and ripple marks. The left lateral margin is thick and with natural cortex serving as backing. The right lateral margin is thin and sharp with use-marks, fresh. (18.5×8.5×2.8mm)

85. A broken backed piece of Chalcedony. Dorsal surface is fully flaked with shallow and deep flake scars. Ventral surface shows primary flake surface with a diffused bulb of percussion. Left lateral margin is thick with cortex serving as backing. Right lateral margin is thin with use-marks, fresh. (19×5.3×2.5mm)

86. A backed piece on a narrow broken blade of Chalcedony. Dorsal surface shows longitudinal ridges with a patch of cortex on the left half. Ventral surface is with ripple marks. The left lateral margin is thick with cortex serving as backing. The right lateral margin thin and with occasional use marks, fresh. (19.1×5.4×3.5mm)

87. A backed piece on thin, slender flake of Chalcedony. Dorsal surface shows a forked median ridge. Ventral surface is primary flake surface and with a tiny bulb. Right lateral margin is slightly thick and serves as natural backing while the left lateral margin is thin and shaped with use-marks, fresh. (21.5×5.5×1.5mm)

88. A broken backed piece on a thick blade of Chalcedony. Upper surface is fully flaked with a high ridge on the right half while the left half is thin and slopes along the edge. Under surface primary, flake surface with a prominent bulb of percussion. The lateral margin is thick and partly flaked, so serves as natural backing. The left lateral margin is thin and sharp with occasional use-marks, fresh. (25×10.3×3.3mm)

89. Backed piece on slightly broken blade of Chalcedony. Dorsal surface fully flaked with high ridge on the right half and with shallow and deep flake scars on the left half. Ventral surface shows a prominent bulb of percussion and primary flake surface. The right lateral margin is thick and shows occasional removal of a few flakes and serves as backing. The left lateral margin is thin and shows use-marks, fresh. (28×13.2×4mm)

90. A backed piece of Carnelian. Dorsal surface shows a median high ridge with a longitudinal cortex patch on the right half. Ventral surface shows primary flake surface with a bulb of percussion. The right lateral margin is thick with cortex serving as backing while the left lateral margin is thin and shows use-marks, fresh. (32×9.2×4mm)

91. Thick backed piece of Chert broken at the distal end, has median ridge on the dorsal surface. Primary flake surface with no traces of bulb on the ventral surface. Left lateral margin is steeply blunted. Whole the right lateral margin is minutely retouched to serve cutting purpose, fresh. (33×15×6mm)

92. Thick backed piece of Chert, broken at the distal end. Ridged dorsal surface. Primary flake surface without bulb. Left lateral margin is thick and blunted while the right lateral margin is thin and shows use-marks, fresh. (29×10×5mm)

93. Thick backed piece on broken blade of Carnelian, broken at the distal end. Ridges on the dorsal surface. Ventral surface is primary with a prominent bulb. The left lateral margin is thick and blunted. The right lateral margin is sharp and thin and shows use-marks, fresh. (29×12×6mm)

94. Backed piece of chert. Dorsal surface fully flaked. Ventral surface shows primary flake surface with a bulb of percussion. The left lateral margin is thick and steeply blunted. The right lateral margin is thin and minutely retouched, fresh. (27×7.3×4.7mm)

95. Backed piece on a thick and broad blade of chert. Dorsal surface fully flaked with deep and shallow flake scars, and is thick at the distal end. Ventral surface with primary flake surface with bulbar scars. The right lateral margin is comparatively thick and shows steep minute working continued to the distal end. The left lateral margin is thin and shows with use-marks, fresh. (31×15.5×5.5mm)

96. Backed piece on backed piece of Carnelian, dorsal surface is fully flaked with small shallow and deep flake scars. Ventral surface shows a prominent bulb of percussion and ripple marks. The right lateral margin is thick and with bold retouch, the left lateral margin is thin and for cutting purpose shows use marks, fresh. (35.5×14×4.5mm)

97. Backed piece on narrow thick blade of banded Agate, fully flaked dorsal surface; primary flake surface with a small bulb of percussion on the ventral surface right lateral margin is partly flaked and partly steeply blunted, left lateral margin is thin and shows use marks, fresh. (37.4×6.5×3.5mm)

98. Backed piece on thick and slightly irregular blade of chert, dorsal surface is fully flaked, ventral surface shows ripple marks, right lateral margin is steeply blunted, left lateral margin is thin and shows use marks, fresh. (45.4×5.5×4mm)

99. Thick and narrow backed piece on blade of Chalcedony, dorsal surface shows a median high ridge, ventral surface primary flake surface with a bulbar scar, one of the lateral margin is steeply blunted and its opposite margin shows use-marks, fresh. (44.5×5.5×4mm)

100. Backed piece on a blade of Cherty Carnelian dorsal surface fully flaked ventral

surface primary one of the lateral margins is thick and blunted, the opposite margin shows use-marks, fresh. (32×8.5×3.5mm)

101. Backed piece on a thick broken piece of Chalcedony both the surfaces are fully flaked, one of the lateral margins is steeply worked to get blunted edge and the opposite margin is thin and shows use-marks, fresh. (25.7×8.7×5.8mm)

102. Backed piece on a thick narrow blade of Carnelian, fully flaked dorsal surface, primary flake surface with a bulb of percussion on the ventral surface, the left lateral margin is steeply worked, the right lateral margin is thir and shows use marks, fresh. (25.5×8.2×4mm)

103. Broken backed piece of Chalcedony, dorsal surface shows a forked ridge, ventral surface is primary flake surface. Left lateral margin is thick with steep blunting the opposite margin is comparatively thin and shows minute retouch, fresh. (23×7×4.4mm)

104. Slightly broken thick backed piece of narrow blade of chert, dorsal surface with median high ridge, ventral surface is fully flaked. One of the lateral margins are steeply worked and blunted to get edge, it's opposite margin is thin and shows use-marks, fresh. (27.1×6.5×4.3mm)

105. Thin backed piece on a small blade of Carnelian, dorsal surface shows a median ridge, ventral surface shows a primary flake surface with a bulb of percussion the right lateral margin shows steep blunting towards the distal end, while the left lateral margin is thin and shows use marks, fresh. (26.8×8.8×3mm)

106. A backed piece on a broken thick blade of Chert. Dorsal surface shows a longitudinal ridge, ventral surface with primary flaked surface. Distal end broken. Lateral margin shows thick steep flaking to obtain blunt edge. Right lateral margin is thin and shows use-marks, fresh. (27×7.7×4.2mm)

107. A backed piece on narrow thick blade of Carnelian, dorsal surface shows a median high ridge, ventral surface shows a primary flake surface with a bulb of percussion. The left lateral margin is steeply blunted; right lateral margin shows occasional use marks, fresh. (23.4×5×3mm)

108. Backed piece on thick broken blade of Chalcedony, dorsal surface shows a forked ridge, ventral shows with primary flake surface, one of the lateral margin is thick and with steep blunted, its opposite margin is thin and short and with minute retouch, fresh. (20×8×4mm)

109. Backed piece on narrow blade of broken Carnelian, dorsal surface shows two parallel ridges, ventral surface shows primary flake surface, one of the lateral margins

with excellent steep blunting. Its opposite margin is thin and shows used marks, fresh. (20.7×6.6×3mm)

110. Backed piece on broken and narrow blade of banded Agate, dorsal surface fully flaked, ventral surface primary, flake surface. One of the lateral margins shows steep blunting, the opposite margin is thin and shows use marks, fresh. (20×5×3mm)

111. Backed piece on broken narrow blade. Dorsal surface shows two parallel ridges, ventral surface shows primary flake surface, one of the lateral margins is steeply blunted and its opposite lateral margin shows excellent minute retouch, fresh. (15×6×3mm)

112. Slightly broken backed piece on a narrow blade of Carnelian, dorsal surface fully flaked, ventral surface with primary flake surface, one of the lateral margins is thick and steeply blunted, the opposite margin is thin and shows use-marks, fresh. (22.2×6×3mm)

113. A backed piece on thick blade of Chalcedony, dorsal and ventral surfaces are fully flaked, one of the lateral margins is thick and steeply blunted, its opposite margin is thin and shows use marks, fresh. (21×6.8×4.2mm)

114. A backed piece on blade of chert, dorsal and ventral surfaces are fully flaked, one of the lateral margins is thick with excellent steep blunting, its opposite margin is thin and shows use marks, fresh. (26×8×4mm)

115. Paralleled blade of jasper, dorsal surface contains irregular ridges with shallow and deep flake scars on the left half, sloppy surface on the right half, ventral surface shows primary flake surface with a bulbar scar. On the left lateral margin at the distal end a deep flake scar is removed to obtain concavity. The later is steeply blunted perhaps for grip or for hafting, use –marks are found on its opposite margin (right) and also on a part of the left lateral margin below the blunted edges, fresh. (39×10×5mm)

116. A parallel sided blade of Chert with two parallel median ridges on the upper surface, primary flake surface on the ventral surface, distal end slightly broken. A part of the left lateral margin is thick and blunted by excellent steep flaking perhaps for grip hand to hold or for hafting extending to 3/4th of the length from proximal end. The right lateral margin shows use marks, fresh. (37×10×3.2mm)

117. A broad blade of Chalcedony a median forked ridge on the dorsal surface. Primary flake surface on the ventral surface. The left lateral margin is steeply blunted and minutely worked. A part of the lateral margin extending from proximal end for hand-grip. Middle portion is steeply minutely blunted and the rest of the margin is sharp and shows use marks. The broad distal end is also blunted. The right lateral margin shows use marks, fresh. (32×15×4mm)

118. A pointed small thin flake of Carnelian, a longitudinal forked ridge on the upper surface, the primary flake surface with a prominent bulb of percussion and a bulbar scar with a facetted platform on the under surface. Excellent minute blunting is noticed on a portion of the right lateral margin near the distal end. Left lateral margin shows occasional use-marks, fresh. (21×9×2.5mm)

119. A pointed blade of Chalcedony with two irregular ridges on the dorsal surface, primary flake surface and a small bulb of percussion on the ventral surface; the left lateral margin is steeply blunted and especially concentrated on the upper half of the tool. The margin is narrowing to a blunt point while the right lateral margin shows use-marks, fresh. (28×11.5×4.2mm)

120. Penknife blade (tranchet) on Chalcedony, upper surface shows a median ridge, under surface shows primary flake surface with flake scars along one of the margin. Right lateral margin is steeply and minutely blunted extending to the broad distal end while the left lateral margin shows use-marks and also retouch near the proximal end, fresh. (28.6×10×4.1mm)

121. Penknife blade (tranchet) of Chalcedony, upper surface shows deep and small flake scars forming parallel ridges under surface is primary flake surface with bulb of percussion. The right lateral margin is comparatively thick steep blunting is noticed on the distal end converging into the point with the left lateral margin. Left lateral margin is thin, sharp and shows use-marks, fresh. (29×11×4mm)

122. Tranchet on a small thin broad blade of Chalcedony. Dorsal surface shows many irregular small ridges, ventral surface shows bulbar scar and ripple marks. Steep minute working result in blunting is noticed at the distal end. Occasional use-marks on the straight left lateral margin, fresh. (21×9×3mm)

123. Side scraper on thick core flake of Agate; steep flaking on one of longitudinal margin to obtain scraping edge, fresh. (35×14×10mm)

124. Side scraper on narrow end flake of Chalcedony, upper surface shows shallow and deep flake scars. Under surface shows primary flake surface with a bulb of percussion, steep flaking on the left lateral margin to obtain scraping edge, fresh. (33×14×5.5mm)

125. Side scraper on a thick flake of chert, upper surface shows deep and shallow flake scars, forming irregular ridge, under surface shows primary flake surface, the right lateral margin is steeply flaked to obtain scraping edge, fresh. (28×14.2×6mm)

126. Side scraper on a thick broken blade of chert, dorsal surface shows a long shallow flake scar and a few small deep flake scars near proximal end, ventral surface shows primary flake surface with a prominent bulb of percussion. The right lateral margin

is thick and partly flaked for grip to hold the left lateral margin is comparatively thin and shows steep minute flaking to obtain scraping edge, fresh. (23.5×11.4×6mm)

127. Side scraper on a very thick rectangular broken flake of Carnelian. Upper surface shows a high thick median ridge with sloppy surfaces on either side, under surface is partly flaked especially near the proximal end and along one lateral margin, scraping edge is obtained on the left lateral margin by steep flaking from the under surface, fresh. (23×15×13mm)

BOARD IV

128. Double side scraper on a broad broken blade of chert, dorsal surface fully flaked with shallow and deep flake scars, ventral surface shows primary flake surface with a large bulbar scar and prepared platform, both the lateral margins are steeply flaked to obtain scraping edge, fresh. (27.4×21×9mm)

129. Double side cum end scraper on a broken thick blade of chert, dorsal surface shows a median longitudinal ridge with small shallow and deep small flake scars. Ventral surface is partly flaked with a prominent bulb and bulbar scar, right lateral margin is steeply flaked from dorsal surface extending to the distal end, while the left lateral margin is steeply flaked on the ventral surface to obtain scraping edges, fresh. (19×22.4×10mm)

130. Double side cum end scraper on a rectangular broad broken blade of chert. Upper surface shows small shallow and deep small flake scars, under surface shows primary flake surface with a bulb of percussion, both the lateral margins and at the distal end are steeply flaked to obtain scraping edges, fresh. (25.5×20.5×6mm)

131. End scraper on a rough triangular thick flake core of Agate, upper surface shows high irregular ridges with shallow and deep flake scars, under surface is partly flaked and show ripple marks. The broader distal end is steeply flaked to obtain scraping edge, fresh. (21.6×31.4×15mm)

132. An end scraper on an irregular long flake of chert, upper surface is fully flaked, under surface is partly flaked with traces of bulb of percussion. The distal end is steeply worked from ventral surface to obtain scraping edge, fresh. (33×18.6×8mm)

133. An end scraper on a flake blade of chert, dorsal surface shows a median high ridge with minute flaking on the left half. Ventral surface shows the primary flaking surface with bulb and bulbar scar, the distal end is steeply flaked from dorsal surface to obtain scraping edge; the right lateral margin is thin and shows use marks, fresh. (28×16.4×5.5mm)

134. An end scraper on a triangular thick flake of chert, dorsal surface shows many irregular high ridges with shallow and deep flake scars, ventral surface shows

primary flake surface with two bulbs of percussion, the distal end shows steep minute flaking from dorsal surface to obtain scraping edge, fresh. (22.6×26.2×6.6mm)

135. Side cum end scraper on thick and broad broken blade of chert, dorsal surface fully flaked, ventral surface primary flake surface with a prominent bulb of percussion and a prepared platform. Steep flaking is noticed on the distal end and the left lateral margin to obtain scraping edges, fresh. (24.5×20×8mm)

136. Side cum end scraper on a squarish thick flake of Agate, upper surface fully flaked; under surface shows primary flake surface with a prominent bulb and bulbar scar and also a prepared platform. Both the lateral margins and the distal end are steeply worked to obtain the scarping edges, fresh. (25×23×10mm)

137. Side cum end scraper on thick irregular small flake of chert, upper surface fully flaked with shallow and deep flake scars; under surface shows primary flake surface with a bulb of percussion and a bulbar scar. Both the lateral margins and the distal end are steeply flaked to obtain scraping edges, fresh. (21×21×8mm)

138. Side cum end scraper on roughly rectangular flake of Chalcedony, dorsal surface shows the median high forked ridge with shallow and deep small flake scars, under surface shows ripple marks at broader distal end along the right lateral margin steep flaking is noticed to obtain scraping edges, fresh. (30.5×19.6×8mm)

139. Side cum end scraper on a irregular flake of chert, upper surface shows irregular ridges with shallow and deep flake scars, under surface shows primary flake surface with no traces of bulb or bulb of percussion. The left lateral margin and the distal end are steeply flaked to obtain scraping edge The right lateral margin is thin and shows use marks, fresh. (29×21×9mm)

140. Side cum end scraper on a thick rectangular flake of Chalcedony. Dorsal surface shows two parallel ridges running wide apart with shallow and deep flake scars. Under surface shows primary flake scars with a prominent bulb and a bulbar scar and a facetted striking platform, the left lateral margin and the distal end are steeply minutely flaked to obtain scraping edges, fresh. (26.4×16.2×5mm)

141. Side cum end scraper on thick rectangular flake of Carnelian, dorsal surface shows median high ridge with sloppy surfaces on either side, ventral surface shows a primary flake surface with a prominent bulb of percussion. The left lateral margin and the distal end are steeply flaked to obtain scraping edge, right lateral margin shows used marks, fresh. (22.4×16×7mm)

142. Round scraper on a ovalish flake of Agate, dorsal surface shows small deep scars and shallow flake scars forming irregular ridges, ventral surface shows primary

flake surface with a prominent bulb of percussion and a faceted striking platform, steep flaking all along the periphery, fresh. (26.2×18×7mm)

143. Crescent shaped thick flake of chert; dorsal surface is fully flaked with a patch of cortex, ventral surface with primary flake surface, steep flaking all along the periphery to obtain scraping edge, fresh. (17.5×28×10mm)

144. Irregular shaped flake of Carnelian, with dorsal surface shows a forked ridge with a shallow and deep flake scars ventral surface shows primary flake surface with a bulb of percussion and bulbar scars, steep flaking all along the periphery to obtain scraping edge, fresh. (15.5×22.3×6mm)

145. Ovalish flake of chert, dorsal surface shows a ridge with a deep and shallow flake scars, ventral surface shows primary flake surface with a bulb of percussion, steep flaking all along the periphery to obtain scraping edge, fresh. (21×19×6.5mm)

146. Roughly triangular shaped flake chert, dorsal surface shows many deep and shallow flake scars, ventral surface shows primary flake surface with a prominent bulb of percussion, steep flaking all along the periphery, fresh. (22×27×10mm)

BOARD V

147. Side cum hollow scraper on a roughly rectangular flake of chert, the left lateral margin and the narrow proximal end are steeply flaked to obtain scraping edge. The right lateral margin is minutely flaked to obtain concave scraping edge, dorsal surface is thick on the left half and slopes towards the right lateral margin, fresh. (26×19×13.5)

148. Hollow scraper cum borer on a thick irregular flake of Agate. Upper surface shows a high median ridge with a large deep flake scar sloping towards right lateral margin and many small shallow and deep flake scars on the left half. Under surface flaked all along the periphery leaving a large central primary surface, left lateral margin is steeply worked with a projection to use as borer, while on the right lateral margin hollow is created and followed by minute flaking on the under surface to obtain concave scraping edges, fresh. (30×25.5×13mm)

149. Hollow cum side scraper on irregular flake of Carnelian, fully flaked upper surface with small shallow and deep flake scars. Under surface shows primary flake surface with traces of a bulb of percussion, left lateral margin is steeply worked to obtain scraping edge, on the right lateral margin a large and shallow hollow is created from under side followed by minute flaking to obtain concave scraping edge, fresh. (23.5×22.5×9mm)

150. Double hollow cum side scraper on thick irregular flake of Chert. Upper surface is fully flaked. Under surface shows primary flake surface with a prominent bulb of percussion. Two hollow scraping edges are obtained on the right lateral margin of

distal end by creating of a shallow and large hollow and followed by minute flaking, the left lateral margin is steeply worked from under side to obtain scraping edge, fresh. (31×23×8mm)

151. Side cum end and hollow scraper on a thick flake of Jasper, scraping edge is obtained on the left lateral margin and at the distal end by steep flaking. On the right lateral margin and shallow large is created and followed by minute flaking to obtain a concave scraping edge, fresh. (32×23.5×10mm)

152. A hollow scraper on a crescent flake of chert, upper surface partly flaked, under surface shows primary. Flake surface with traces of a bulb on the left lateral margin a shallow and large and hollow is created and followed by minute flaking to obtain scraping edge, fresh. (36×13×12.5mm)

153. A hollow cum side scraper of Carnelian, upper surface shows irregular ridges with shallow and deep flake scars, under surface shows a prominent bulb of percussion with ripple marks and a prepared striking platform; both the margins show scraping edges obtained by steep flaking. Shallow scraping edge is obtained on the left lateral margin towards proximal end by the removal of shallow and small flake and followed by minute flaking inside the hollow, fresh. (28×20×7mm)

154. A hollow scraper on a pointed long blade of Carnelian. Dorsal surface shows forked two parallel longitudinal ridges with shallow and deep flake scars, ventral surface is primary, flake surface with a bulbar scar right lateral margin is minutely retouched, left lateral margin shows use-marks and a notch near the distal end made on the ventral surface, fresh. (47.5×12×4.5mm)

155. A hollow scraper on a slightly broken blade of Carnelian, dorsal surface shows a median forked high ridge with shallow and deep flake scars on the left half and longitudinal shallow flake scars on right half. Ventral surface is primary flake surface, with broken proximal end. On the left lateral margin a shallow hollow is created and followed by minute flaking on the dorsal surface to obtain a hollow scraping edge. Right lateral margin shows occasional use-marks, fresh. (36×10.5×4.5mm)

156. A notched scraper on pointed blade of Agate dorsal surface shows a high median forked ridge, ventral surface shows a prominent bulb of percussion and ripple marks and a facetted striking platform left lateral margin show use-marks. On the right lateral margin a shallow hollow is obtained by removal of a shallow flake on the ventral surface and followed by minute flaking at the distal end, fresh. (28×11×5mm)

157. Scraper on a residual conical fluted core Agate, steep flaking is noticed on broader transverse edge to obtain scraping edge, fresh. (41×36.8×13.5mm)

158. Scraper on a fragment of conical fluted core of chert, steep flaking is noticed on lateral margin to obtain scraping edge, fresh. (38×23×11.5mm)

159. Scraper on elongated oval fluted core of Chalcedony, steep flaking is visible on broader transverse edge to obtain scraping edge, fresh. (44×29×14.6mm)

160. Scraper on residual conical shaped fluted core of chert; the broader transverse edge is steeply flaked to obtain scraping edge, fresh. (42×20.5×12.5mm)

161. Scraper on a fragment of conical shaped fluted core of Carnelian, its broader transverse edge is steeply flaked to obtain scraping edge, fresh. (46×18.5×15mm)

162. Scraper on a fragment of a core of jasper, its broader transverse edge is steeply flaked to obtain scraping edge, fresh. (38.5×21.4×8mm)

163. Scraper on a fragment of fluted core of Agate, steep flaking is visible along a part of th4e periphery to obtain scraping edge, fresh. (31×20×15mm)

164. Scraper on a fragment of fluted core of Chalcedony, steep flaking is observed on a part of the periphery to obtain scraping edge, fresh. (20×17×12mm)

165. Scraper on fragment of a core of jasper, steep flaking is noticed on longer margin to obtain scraping edge, fresh. (13×25×18mm)

166. Borer cum scraper on a narrow thick flake of jasper, borer point is obtained at the distal end by minute working on either margins, the right lateral margin is steeply flaked to obtain a scraping edge, fresh. (47.6×13×3mm)

167. Borer cum scraper on a thick irregular core flake of chert, borer point is obtained at the distal end by steep flaking on either margins, both the lateral margins are also steeply worked to obtain scraping edge, semi rolled. (32×22.5×11.5m)

168. Fragment of a core of narrow blade of crystal. A core point is obtained by minute flaking on either margin; under surface is with primary flake surface, fresh. (15.5×5×3.5mm)

169. A core on a pointed end flake of Agate, dorsal surface shows a median ridge forked at intervals with shallow and deep flake scars. Ventral surface is primary flake surface with a prominent bulb of percussion and facetted striking platform. A core point is obtained at the distal end by minute working on lateral margins, fresh. (29.5×11.4×4.4mm)

BOARD VI

170. Crescent point on a thin and very slender blade of opal, the arc is convex and is blunted by excellent steep minute work. The card is straight and shows use-marks making a point with retouched arc. Dorsal surface shows a median ridge, ventral surface shows ripple marks, fresh. (22×5×2mm)

171. Crescent point on a slender blade of Chalcedony, the arc is convex and shows excellent steep retouch, the chord is straight and shows occasional use-marks making a

point with the arc at the distal end. Dorsal surface shows a median high ridge, ventral surface primary flake surface with traces of a bulb, fresh. (21.5×5×3mm)

172. Crescent point on a slender slightly broken blade of Chalcedony, the arc is convex and shows excellent steep retouch, the chord is straight and shows use-marks, chord making a point with the arc at the distal end. Dorsal surface is fully flaked and ventral surface is primary, fresh. (22.5×6×3.7mm)

173. Crecentic point on a narrow thick blade of Chalcedony, the arc is convex and shows excellent steep retouch, the chord is straight and with use-marks, making a point with the retouched arc at the distal end. The ventral surface is primary, fresh. (24×6.5×4mm)

174. Broken crescent point on a slender blade of Chalcedony, the arc is convex and shows excellent steep retouch, the chord is straight and shows use-marks making a point with the arc at the distal end. Dorsal and ventral surface is primary, fresh. (25×5.5×3mm)

175. Crescent point on a slender blade of crystal, the arc is convex and shows excellent steep retouch, the chord is roughly straight and shows use-marks. The chord makes a point with the retouched arc at the distal end; upper surface shows a longitudinal ridge running close to the arc, lower surface shows primary flake surface with a bulb, fresh. (22.8×5.5×2.5mm)

176. A crescent point on a slender blade of Chalcedony, the arc is convex and shows excellent steep minute retouch, the chord is straight and shows use marks; The chord makes a point with the arc at the distal end, ventral surface is primary, fresh. (29×6×2.5mm)

177. Broken crescent point on a slender blade of crystal, the arc is convex and shows excellent steep retouch, the chord is roughly straight and shows use-marks. The chord makes a point with the retouched arc at one end; dorsal surface shows a median ridge, ventral surface is primary, fresh. (21.4×8×2mm)

178. Crescent point on a slender blade of Carnelian, the arc is convex and shows excellent steep retouch, the chord is straight and shows use-marks. The chord makes a point with the retouched arc on the distal end; dorsal surface shows a longitudinal ridge, ventral surface shows primary flake surface with no traces of bulb, fresh. (29×6×2.5mm)

179. A broken crescent point on Carnelian, the arc is convex and shows excellent steep retouch, the chord is straight and shows use-marks making a point with the retouched arc at the distal end; dorsal surface shows a ridge, ventral surface primary with missing of proximal end, fresh. (21×6.5×3mm)

180. A Crescent point on a narrow blade of Chalcedony. The arc is convex and

shows steep minute retouch, the chord is almost straight and shows use-marks making a point with the retouched arc at the distal end; dorsal surface flaked with a forked ridge, ventral surface shows primary flake surface and a bulb of percussion, fresh. (33.5×7.5×3.7mm)

181. A crescent point on chert, the arc is convex and shows excellent blunting, the chord is straight and shows use-marks. The chord makes a point with the retouched arc at the distal end; dorsal surface shows a ridge running close to the arc, sloping to the right lateral ventral surface primary, fresh. (46.6×8×4mm)

182. Micro burin on used blade of opal upper surface shows two parallel longitudinal ridges. Ventral surface is primary with no traces of bulb. Burin edge is obtained at the distal end by the removal of a vertical spall on the left lateral margin and minute blunting is noticed at the proximal end on the same margin perhaps for hold; the right lateral margin shows use marks, fresh. (25×8.5×3.4mm)

183. Burin on a used thin broken and pointed blade of Chalcedony, dorsal surface shows irregular ridges with shallow and deep flake scars. Ventral surface primary proximal end is missing, burin edge is obtained at the broken end of the blade by removal of a vertical spall on one of the margins opposite to sharp blade edge with use marks, fresh. (22×10×3mm)

184. Burin on a broken backed blade of Chalcedony, dorsal surface shows three longitudinal ridges with large shallow and small deep flake scars in between. Ventral surface primary with a bulb of percussion, the right lateral margin shows steep minute flaking, while the left lateral margin shows use marks near the proximal end and a burin edge at the broken part of the distal end. Burin edge is obtained by the removal of a vertical spall on the left lateral margin near the distal end, fresh. (26.5×8×4mm)

185. Burin on a broken used blade of Chalcedony, dorsal surface shows small shallow and deep flake scars forming irregular ridges. Ventral surface primary with ripple marks near the broken part of the blade where burin edge is obtained. Burin edge is created on the broader end of the blade by the removal of a vertical spall on one of the lateral margins. Use marks are visible on the same margin slightly below the spall on narrowing end, fresh. (31×9×3mm)

BOARD VII

186. Lunates on thick long blade of Chalcedony, upper surface shows median ridge, under surface primary with a bulb of percussion, the arc is convex and shows excellent steep working (blunting), the chord is straight shows use marks, fresh. (38×11.5×4.5mm)

187. Lunate on small and thin blade of Carnelian, upper surface shows a forked

ridge with shallow and deep flake scars, under surface primary with no traces of bulb, the arc is convex and shows excellent steep working to get blunted edge, the chord is straight and shows minute retouch, fresh. (28.5×9.5×4mm)

188. Lunate on a small flake of chert, upper surface shows a small longitudinal ridge close to arc. Under surface primary, the arc is convex and shows blunting by steep flaking, the chord is roughly straight and shows use marks, fresh. (19×8.7×3mm)

189. Lunate on a thick irregular blade of Chalcedony, dorsal surface shows a forked ridge with shallow and deep flake scars. Ventral surface primary, the arc is slightly convex and shows excellent blunting, the chord is roughly straight and shows use marks, fresh. (34.6×10.5×5mm)

190. Lunate on a slender thin blade of Carnelian. Dorsal surface shows a small longitudinal ridge close to the arc, the ventral surface primary, the arc is convex and shows excellent steep minute flaking to obtain blunted edge, the chord is roughly straight with excellent minute retouch to obtain sharp cutting edge, fresh. (29×6×3mm)

191. Small Lunate on a slender thin blade of crystal. Dorsal surface shows a longitudinal ridge close to the arc, ventral surface primary, the arc is convex and shows excellent steep flaking to obtain blunted edge, the chord is straight and shows use marks, fresh. (21×6×2.5mm)

192. Lunate on a blade of Carnelian, dorsal surface shows a small longitudinal ridge very close to the arc, ventral surface primary, the arc is convex and shows excellent steep flaking to obtain blunted edge, the chord is straight and shows use marks, fresh. (24×9×3mm)

193. A triangle of banded Agate, both the side arms are steeply blunted, the chord is straight and shows use marks. The dorsal surface shows a forked longitudinal ridge, ventral surface is primary with traces of bulb, fresh. (33.5×9×3.5mm)

194. A triangular small blade of Agate, both the side arms are steeply blunted, the chord is straight and shows occasional use marks. The dorsal surface shows a small longitudinal ridge very nearer to the blunted edge, ventral surface is primary flake surface with traces of bulb, fresh. (19×7×2.5mm)

195. Asymmetric triangle on a small narrow blade of Chalcedony, dorsal surface shows a small longitudinal ridge, the ventral surface is primary, both the side arms of the triangle are steeply and minutely worked to obtain blunted edges, chord is straight and shows occasional use marks, fresh. (18×5×2.5mm)

196. Asymmetric triangle on a irregular flake of Chalcedony, both the side arms are steeply worked to obtain blunted edges. The chord is straight and shows retouch, the

dorsal surface shows small ridge near blunted margin with shallow and deep flake scars, ventral surface is primary with a bulbar scar at one end, fresh. (25×11.5×4mm)

197. Asymmetrical triangle on a flake of Carnelian, the unequal side arms is steeply worked to obtain blunted edges. The chord is straight and sharp and shows minute retouch, the dorsal surface shows a small ridge, ventral surface is primary, fresh. (28×14×4mm)

198. A symmetric triangle on a flake of chert, both the side arms are steeply flaked to obtain excellent blunted edge. The chord is straight and sharp and shows use marks, the upper surface shows shallow and deep flake scars, under surface is primary, fresh. (29×10×4mm)

199. Trapeze on a slender blade of chert, dorsal surface shows a horizontal forked ridge. Ventral surface is primary. The chord is straight and thin and shows minute retouch, its opposite margin comparatively thick. The middle and the side arms are minutely blunted, fresh. (23×8×3mm)

GHANPUR BOARD

1. Conical fluted core on Chalcedony; parallel-sided blades are removed from its body in two directions with a patch of cortex, fresh.

2. Conical fluted core on Quartzite, parallel-sided flutations all around on its body, flat striking platform on one end and pointed on the other end, fresh.

3. Thick-flake core on Carnelian with excellent parallel-sided flutations on dorsal surface, ventral surface is partly flaked with prominent bulb and bulbar scars, fresh.

4. Conical fluted core on jasper, flat striking platform on one end and pointed on the other end, parallel-sided flutations around its body leaving patches of cortex, fresh.

5. Rectangular end flake of Carnelian, dorsal surface shows a forked median high ridge with a patch of cortex at the distal end. Ventral surface shows primary flake surface with a prominent bulb of percussion, left lateral margin shows minute retouch while right lateral margin with occasional use marks.

6. Pointed end flake on a Chalcedony, dorsal surface shows two parallel ridges, running wide apart with shallow and deep flake scars, ventral surface shows primary flake surface with a prominent bulb of percussion, the right lateral margin shows a minute retouch and the left lateral margin shows use marks, fresh.

7. Rectangular-end flake on Carnelian, a median high ridge forked on either end with a patch of cortex at the distal end. Flake surface is primary with a prominent bulb of percussion on the ventral surface. Occasional use marks on both the lateral margins, fresh.

8. An irregular side flake on Chalcedony, dorsal surface is partly flaked with large shallow and deep flake scars, ventral surface shows primary flake surface with a prominent bulb of percussion and a prepared striking platform, the left lateral margin is minutely retouched, fresh.

9. Leaf shaped end flake on Carnelian, dorsal surface shows three irregular longitudinal ridges with shallow and deep flake scars. Ventral surface shows primary flake surface with a prominent bulb of percussion and a prepared striking platform. Occasional retouch is along the periphery, fresh.

10. Side cum end scraper on a thick side flake of Cherty Quartzite. Dorsal surface fully flaked with small deep and shallow flake scars, ventral surface partly flaked with a prominent bulb of percussion, steeply flaked on the right lateral margin on the dorsal surface and proximal end and left lateral margin on the ventral surface to obtain scraping edge, fresh.

11. Side cum end scraper on a thick flake of Quartzite, dorsal surface shows irregular ridges with deep and shallow flake scars, ventral surface is partly flaked with a bulb of percussion, and a prepared striking platform. Steep flaking at the distal end and a part of the right lateral margin from upper surface to obtain scraping edges, fresh.

12. Side cum end scraper on a thick flake of chert, dorsal surface is partly flaked with deep and shallow flake scars; ventral surface is flaked all along the periphery with a bulb of percussion. Steep flaking on both the lateral margins and at the distal end from upper side to obtain scraping edges, fresh.

13. Hollow cum round scraper on a thick end flake of jasper, dorsal surface shows parallel-sided two longitudinal ridges with shallow and deep flake scars; ventral surface is partly flaked with a prominent bulb of percussion. Steep flaking all along the periphery to obtain scraping edges, partly from the under and partly from the upper surface according to convenience, a hollow is made at the distal end and followed by minute working inside the hollow, fresh.

14. Side cum notched scraper on broken blade of Quartzitc; dorsal surface shows a median high ridge, forked on either end. Ventral surface shows primary flake surface with a bulb of percussion and a prepared striking platform, steep flaking on the left lateral margin and at the distal end from the dorsal surface to obtain scraping edges on the right lateral margin a small notch is made from under surface, fresh.

15. Hollow cum round scraper on an irregular flake of chert, upper surface shows deep and shallow flake scars, lower surface shows primary flake surface with no traces of bulb, steep minute flaking all along the entire periphery, from dorsal surface to obtain scraping edge a hollow scraping edge is obtained on the right lateral margin by removing a flake followed by minute steep flaking inside the hollow.

16. Scraper cum borer on irregular end flake of jasper. Upper surface shows shallow and deep flake scars. Under surface shows primary flake surface with a bulb of percussion, steep minute flaking at the broad distal end to obtain scraping edge, borer point is obtained at the distal end by removing a deep flake on left lateral margin followed by minute secondary working, fresh.

17. Scraper on a thick residual core of jasper, steep flaking is noticed on all along the periphery to obtain scraping edge, fresh.

18. Scraper on a residual core of Chalcedony, scraping edge is noticed on a part of the core, fresh.

19. Borer on an irregular flake of chert, steep working all along the periphery, borer point is obtained at one of the ends by minute working on either side. Dorsal and ventral surfaces are partly flaked, fresh.

20. Burin and a thick blade of jasper, burin edge is obtained at the proximal end by removal of a spall on either margin. Use marks are noticed on either lateral margins, fresh.

21. A backed piece on a parallel sided thick blade of chert. Dorsal surface shows two parallel sided ridges, ventral surface primary flake surface with a bulb of percussion, the left lateral margin is thick and shows removal of a longitudinal flake throughout the side, the right lateral margin is thin and shows use marks, fresh.

22. Backed piece on a parallel side blade of Chalcedony. Upper surface shows two longitudinal (parallel) ridges with shallow and deep flake scars, under surface shows primary flake surface with bulb of percussion. The lateral margin is thick and serves as backing, the right lateral margin is thin and shows use- marks, fresh.

23. Backed piece on a parallel sided piece of Chalcedony, upper surface shows two longitudinal ridges, under surface shows primary flaking surface with a trace of bulb of percussion, the left lateral margin is thick and shows excellent blunting, the right lateral margin shows use-marks. Fresh.

24. Backed piece on a thick broken blade of Chalcedony, upper surface shows a median high ridge with a sloping to right lateral margin. Under surface with primary flake surface with a bulb of percussion, the left lateral margin is thick and excellent blunting, while the right lateral margin shows use-marks, fresh.

25. Backed piece on a blade of milky Quartz. Upper surface shows thick right margin and sloping towards left margin; under surface shows primary flake surface with a bulb and bulbar scar. The right lateral margin shows thick and blunting and the left lateral margin shows use marks, fresh.

26. Backed piece on a narrow blade of Chalcedony, upper surface shows two longitudinal parallel sided ridges, under surface shows primary flake surface with a prominent bulb of percussion. The left lateral margin is thick and partly blunted while the right lateral margin shows use marks, fresh.

27. Backed piece on a pointed blade of Carnelian, upper surface shows a high median ridge and sloping towards right margin. Under surface shows primary flaking surface with a bulb. The left lateral margin shows an excellent blunting; the right lateral margin is thin and sharp with use-marks, fresh.

28. Backed piece on a broken blade of Chalcedony. Dorsal surface show a median forked ridge sloping toward left lateral margin. Ventral surface shows primary flake surface with bulbar scar, the right lateral margin shows excellent minute blunting extending to the distal end. The left lateral margin shows thin and shows excellent minute retouch. Incipient tang is noticed at the proximal end, fresh.

29. Crescent point on a broken blade of Carnelian, dorsal surface shows a longitudinal ridge sloping towards right margin, under surface, shows primary flake surface. The left lateral margin is thick with excellent blunting while the right lateral margin is thin and shows occasional use marks. The distal end forms a sharp point, fresh.

30. Crescentic point on a narrow thick blade of Carnelian. The arch thick and convex and shows excellent blunt, while chord is thin and shows use-marks. The chord makes a point with the blunted arch, fresh.

31. Crescentic point on a narrow blade of Chert. Dorsal surface shows two parallel longitudinal ridges, ventral surface shows primary flake surface, the left lateral margin (arch) is convex with excellent minute blunting, the right lateral margin, (chord) is straight and making a point with the arch and shows use marks, fresh.

32. Crescent point on a narrow blade of Chalcedony. Dorsal surface shows a median high ridge, while the ventral surface shows primary flake surface, the right lateral margin which is slightly convex is minutely blunted, the left lateral margin is straight with use – marks and makes a sharp point with the right lateral margin, fresh.

33. Lunate on a small blade of Carnelian, the arc is steeply blunted and the chord is straight and shows use-marks. The dorsal surface shows a longitudinal ridge, the ventral surface shows primary flake surface, fresh.

34. Lunate on small broad blade of Chalcedony, the arc is thick and steeply blunted the chord is straight and shows use-marks, dorsal surface shows long shallow and deep flake scars, ventral surface shows primary flake surface, fresh.

35. Parallel-sided broken blade of Chalcedony, dorsal surface shows two parallel-sided longitudinal ridges with sloping to margins. Ventral surface shows primary flake

surface, the left lateral margin shows minute retouch and the right lateral margin shows use-marks, fresh.

36. A parallel-sided broken blade of Chalcedony, dorsal surface shows a longitudinal median ridge with sloping on either margin. Ventral surface shows primary flake surface. One of the margins shows excellent minute retouch, fresh.

37. A small parallel-sided blade of Chalcedony, dorsal surface shows a high median ridge, ventral surface shows primary flake surface, with a bulb. Left lateral margin shows excellent minute retouch while right lateral margin shows the use-marks, fresh.

38. Parallel-sided broad blade on Agate, dorsal surface shows a high median ridge, forked on either end, ventral surface shows primary flake surface with ripple marks. Both the lateral margins show minute retouch, fresh.

39. A small broad blade of milky quartz, dorsal surface shows a longitudinal ridge with small, shallow deep scars, ventral surface shows primary flake surface with a bulb of percussion. Both the lateral margins are minutely retouched, fresh.

40. Small narrow blade of Carnelian, dorsal surface shows longitudinal two parallel-sided ridges, ventral surface shows with primary flake surface with bulbar scar. The left lateral margin is minutely retouched. The right lateral margin shows the use-marks, fresh.

41. Pointed blade of Agate, dorsal surface, shows a forked ridge with shallow and deep scar, ventral surface is primary flake surface with bulb of percussion, the left lateral margin shows use-marks, fresh.

42. Parallel-sided blade of Chalcedony, two parallel-sided longitudinal ridges with shallow and deep flake scars on the dorsal surface. Primary flake surface with a prominent bulb of percussion on the ventral surface. Occasional use- marks on either margin, fresh.

43. Parallel sided blade of Quartzite. Dorsal surface shows a forked longitudinal ridge with shallow and deep flake scars. Ventral surface shows primary flake surface with bulb and bulbar scar and prepared striking platform, use-marks on both the margins, fresh.

44. Thick parallel sided blade of Carnelian. Dorsal surface shows two parallel-sided ridges joining at the distal end, with sloping towards the margins. Ventral surface shows primary flaking surface, occasional use-marks are seen on either margin, fresh.

45. Broad thick parallel sided blade of Agate. Dorsal surface shows two longitudinal ridges with sloppy sides. Ventral surface shows primary flake surface without bulb of percussion. Use-marks on either margin, fresh.

46. Long parallel-sided blade of Chalcedony, dorsal surface shows high median ridge with a patch of cortex on the right half of the tool towards the distal end. Ventral surface is shown with primary flake surface, with prominent bulb of percussion and faceted striking platform. The left lateral margin shows use-marks, fresh.

SITAPLALLY(STP)

1. Backed piece on a thick blade of Agate, dorsal surface shows a longitudinal forked ridge with a patch of cortex converging on the left half of the blade. Ventral surface shows primary flake surface with a bulb. The left lateral margin is thick with cortex serving as backing, while the right lateral margin is thin and sharp with use-marks, fresh.

2. Backed piece on a blade of chert, dorsal surface is partly flaked with cortex on the left half of the tool, ventral surface shows primary flake surface, the left lateral margin is thick with cortex serving as back. The right lateral margin is thin with use-marks.

3. Obliquely blunted blade of Agate, dorsal surface shows two longitudinal ridges with shallow and deep flake scars, ventral surface is primary flake surface. The upper part of the right lateral margin is steeply blunted which converges in to point, the left lateral margin which is straight and shows occasional use-marks, fresh.

4. Obliquely blunted blade on Agate, dorsal surface shows irregular forked ridge with small shallow and deep flake scars. Ventral surface shows primary flake surface with a bulb and bulbar scar with ripple marks. The right lateral margin is convex and is steeply blunted on the upper half of the blade. The left lateral margin shows use-marks, fresh.

5. Backed piece on a pointed small broad blade of Agate, dorsal surface shows a forked median ridge with shallow and deep flake scars. Ventral surface shows primary flake surface, the left lateral margin is thick and convex with steep blunting while the right lateral margin is straight and thin with use-marks, fresh.

6. Backed piece on a parallel sided blade of Agate. Dorsal surface shows a longitudinal ridge, ventral surface shows primary flake surface, the left lateral margin is thick with excellent steep working, the right lateral margin is thin and shows use-marks, fresh.

7. A backed piece on pointed small blade of Agate, dorsal surface shows shallow and deep flake scars. Ventral surface shows primary flake surface with bulb removal scar. The right lateral margin shows excellent blunting, while left lateral margin shows occasional use-marks, fresh.

8. Backed piece on a blade of Agate, dorsal surface shows a longitudinal ridge,

ventral surface shows primary flake surface. The left lateral margin is thick and shows excellent blunting, the right lateral margin shows occasional use-marks, fresh.

9. Backed piece on a broken blade of Chalcedony, dorsal surface shows two median parallel ridges with sloppy sides, ventral surface primary flake surface, the left lateral margin and at the distal end are steeply flaked to obtain blunt edges, the right lateral margin is thin and shows use-marks, fresh.

10. Crecentic point on a thin blade of Agate, dorsal surface shows an oblique ridge, ventral surface is primary flake surface, the right lateral margin is thick and convex with excellent blunting, the left lateral margin is thin and sharp and shows use-marks, fresh.

11. Crecentic point on a very thick blade of chert, the dorsal surface shows three irregular ridges with shallow and deep flake scars. The ventral surface shows primary flake surface. The right lateral margin (arch) is thick and shows discontinuous steep blunting while the left lateral margin is straight and making a point with the opposite margin (arch) at the distal end and shows use-marks, fresh.

12. Crecentic point on a broad and thick blade of Agate, the dorsal surface shows a median longitudinal ridge with shallow and deep flake scars. The ventral surface shows primary flake surface with a prominent bulb of percussion and ripple marks and faceted striking platform. The right lateral margin is thick and converging to the distal end shows excellent blunting on the upper half of it, the left lateral margin is thin and use-marks and makes a point with the converging opposite margins, fresh.

13. Crecentic point on a narrow and thick blade of Agate, upper surface is partly flaked. Under surface primary flake surface with traces of a bulb, the left lateral margin is thick and convex and shows excellent blunting, the right lateral margin is thin and straight with use-marks and makes a point with the opposite margin at the distal end, fresh.

14. Lunate on a very thick blade of milky quartz, dorsal surface shows a median ridge and slopes to right margin. Ventral surface shows primary flake surface with no traces of bulb, the arc is thick and convex and shows steep flaking, the chord is thin and straight and shows use-marks, fresh.

15. Lunate on a thick broad blade of milky quartz, dorsal surface shows a median ridge sloping towards right margin, ventral surface primary flake surface with traces of bulb, the arc is convex and thick with excellent blunting, the chord is thin and straight and shows use-marks, fresh.

16. Triangle on a thick small flake of Chalcedony, on dorsal surface a median longitudinal ridge sloping towards right lateral margin. Ventral surface primary flake

surface, the left lateral margin is thick and formed by two facets and is steeply and minutely blunted, the right lateral margin is straight and thin and shows use-marks.

17. Parallel-sided blade of Chalcedony, dorsal surface shows two longitudinal ridges with shallow and deep flake scars, ventral surface shows primary flake surface; one of the margins shows use-marks. A single spall is removed on the left lateral margin of the proximal end, fresh.

18. A broken crecentic point on a small thick blade of Agate. Dorsal surface fully flaked and sloppy towards the left lateral margin, ventral surface primary flake surface, the right lateral margin thick and convex with excellent steep blunting and broken towards posterior end, while the left lateral margin is thin and straight (chord) and makes a point with the arc.

18a. A thick broken blade of banded Agate, dorsal surface shows a high median ridge forked at intervals with shallow and deep flake scars. Ventral surface is primary with traces of a bulb, broken at the distal end, the left lateral margin shows use-marks, fresh.

19. A parallel sided thick and broad blade of Agate, dorsal surface is fully flaked with forked ridge, ventral surface primary flake surface with no traces of bulb and a plain facetted striking platform, both the lateral margin show occasional minute retouch, fresh.

20. A parallel-sided blade of Carnelian, dorsal surface shows two forked longitudinal ridges with shallow and deep flake scars. Ventral surface shows primary flake surface with a prominent bulb of percussion and ripple marks and prepared striking platform, the distal end is thick and occasional use-marks on both the lateral margins, fresh.

POLAVARAM (PVM)

1. Round scraper on thick ovalish flake of milky quartz, upper surface fully flaked, under surface partly flaked with traces of bulb. Steeply flaked all along the periphery to obtain scraping, fresh.

2. Backed piece on broken thick broad blade of milky quartz. Upper surface is partly flaked, and sloping towards right lateral margin. Under surface primary flake surface with prominent bulb of percussion and a prepared striking platform. The left lateral margin is thick unworked serving as natural backing, sight lateral shows, use-marks, distal end broken fresh.

3. Backed piece on a leaf shaped flake of Agate, upper surface shows forked median longitudinal ridge with shallow and deep flake scars, under surface shows traces of a bulb and ripple marks; the left lateral margin is thick and blunted, the right lateral margin shows occasional blunting-fresh.

4. Backed piece on narrow blade of Chalcedony, upper surface shows two narrow longitudinal median ridges running closely, slopping on either margins, under surface primary flake surface, the left lateral margin is minutely steeply blunted, while the right lateral margin shows use-marks, fresh.

5. Small parallel sided thick blade of Agate, upper surface shows a high median forked ridge with shallow and deep flake scars, under surface shows primary flake scars. Occasional used marks on either margins, fresh.

6. Retouched parallel-sided thin blade of rock crystal, dorsal surface shows longitudinal median high ridge with a patch of cortex at the distal end. Ventral surface shows primary flake surface, with primary bulb of percussion. The left lateral margin is minutely retouched, while the right lateral margin shows occasional use-marks, fresh.

7. A small thick parallel-sided blade of milky Quartz, dorsal surface shows two parallel-sided longitudinal ridges, ventral surface shows primary flake surface with a bulb. Proximal end broken- fresh.

8. A thick parallel sided blade of milky Quartz. Dorsal surface shows a high median ridge with shallow and deep flake scars, ventral surface shows a prominent bulb of percussion. The left lateral margin has occasional use marks, fresh.

CUDDAPAH (GVS)

1. Double-sided scraper on narrow thick blade of Lidionite, dorsal surface shows two parallel-sided ridges, joining at proximal end. Ventral surface shows primary flake surface with a bulb of percussion. Both the lateral margins are steeply flaked to obtain scraping edges, fresh.

2. Backed piece on narrow thin blade of Lydionite, dorsal surface partly flaked; ventral surface shows primary flake surface. The left lateral margin is thick and serves as backing, while the right lateral margin is thin and shows occasional use marks.

3. Backed piece on a broad thick blade of Quartzite, dorsal surface shows a longitudinal median forked ridge, ventral surface shows primary flake surface with traces of bulb, the left lateral margin is thick, steeply blunted, the right lateral margin is thin and retouched, fresh.

4. Backed piece on a narrow thin blade of Lydionite, dorsal surface shows irregular ridges with shallow and deep flake scars with a bulbar scar, the left lateral margin is minutely blunted, while the right lateral margin shows use-marks, fresh.

5. A crescent point on a narrow pointed blade of Lydionite. The upper surface is partly flaked with sloppy surface towards right side, the lower surface is primary flake surface, the left lateral margin is thick and convex with excellent blunting, the right

lateral margin is thin and straight with use-marks and making a point with the opposite margin, fresh.

6. A crescent point on broad thick blade of Cherty Quartzite, dorsal surface shows a median longitudinal ridge sloping to left lateral margin, ventral surface shows primary flake surface and broken at the proximal end. The right lateral margin and thick and convex with steep blunting, while the left lateral margin is thin and straight with use-marks and makes a point with the arc, fresh.

7. Broken Lunate on a broad thick pointed blade of chert. Dorsal surface shows two parallel sided longitudinal ridges with shallow and deep flake scars, the ventral surface shows primary flake surface. The right lateral margin is thick with excellent blunting, the left lateral margin is thin and straight with use-marks, fresh.

8. Lunate on a thick narrow blade of Lydionite, dorsal surface shows a median ridge, ventral surface shows primary flake surface. The arc is thick and steeply blunted, while the chord is straight and shows occasionally use-marks, fresh.

9. Lunate on a thick small blade of Quartzite, dorsal surface is fully flaked; ventral surface shows primary flake surface. The arc is thick with steep blunting; the chord is straight and shows occasionally use-marks, fresh.

10. Broken parallel sided blade on Lydionite. The dorsal surface shows the longitudinal ridges, ventral surface shows primary flake surface with a bulb. The right lateral margin shows occasional use-marks, fresh.

CHENNARAOPET (CRP)

1. Side scraper on pointed core flake of chert. The dorsal surface shows a high median ridge with shallow and deep flake scars, ventral surface shows primary flake surface with traces of bulb. The left lateral margin towards distal end is steeply, minutely flaked to obtain scraping edge, fresh.

2. Scraper on a residual fluted core of chert. Steep minute flaking is noticed on one of the margins to obtain scraping edge, fresh.

3. Double sided cum end scraper on broad blade of Chalcedony, dorsal surface shows three longitudinal ridges with shallow deep flake scars. Ventral surface shows primary flake scars with traces of bulb and prepared striking platform, the scraping edge is obtained on both the lateral margins and at the distal end by minute steep flaking, fresh.

4. Notched scrapper on an irregular flake of Chalcedony, upper surface shows two ridges with shallow and deep flake scars and patch of cortex at the distal end. Under surface is primary flake surface with a prominent bulb of percussion. A notch is obtained

on the left lateral margin by removing a deep flake on the under surface, while therc is an attempt of blunting on the right lateral margin from upper surface, fresh.

5. A backed piece on a thick broken blade of Chalcedony, upper surface shows a longitudinal high ridge sloping towards right lateral margins, under surface primary flake surface with a prepared striking platform. The left lateral margin is thick and serves as blunting, while the right lateral margin is thin and shows use-marks.

6. A backed piece on a small blade of jasper, dorsal surface shows a forked ridge with shallow and deep flake scar. Ventral surface shows primary flake surface with a prominent bulb of percussion and ripple marks; the right lateral margin is thick and natural surface serves as backing, while the left lateral margin is thin and shows use-marks, fresh.

7. Backed piece on a small blade of Chalcedony, dorsal surface is partly flaked with a patch of cortex on the left lateral margins. A ventral surface shows primary flake surface with a prominent bulb of percussion and a prepared striking platform.

8. Backed piece on thick blade of opal dorsal surface shows shallow and deep flake scars forming irregular ridges. Ventral surface shows primary flake surface with a bulb of percussion. The right lateral margin is thick and serves as natural backing while the left lateral margin is thin and shows occasional use-marks, fresh.

9. Backed piece on thin blade of jasper. Dorsal surface shows a longitudinal median ridge and shallow deep scars, ventral surface is primary flake surface with a bulb of percussion and ripple marks. The left lateral margin is comparatively thick and shows occasional blunting which serves as blunted force, while the right lateral margin shows use-marks, fresh.

10. Backed piece on thick blade of Quartzite, dorsal surface fully flaked, ventral surface shows primary flake surface, with no trace of bulb. The right lateral margin is thick with steep minute flaking; the left lateral margin is thin and shows use-marks, fresh.

11. Backed piece on narrow thin blade of Jasper. Dorsal surface shows a median longitudinal ridge with shallow and deep flake scars. Ventral surface shows primary flake surface with a bulb, the right lateral margin is comparatively thick with minute blunting, the left lateral margin is thin and shows retouch, fresh.

12. Backed piece on a narrow thick blade of Chalcedony, dorsal surface shows partly flaked with shallow and deep flake scars, ventral surface is primary flake surface with bulb of percussion. The right lateral margin is thick with steep blunting, while the left lateral margin is thin and shows use-marks, fresh.

13. Crescentic point on a thick blade of Chalcedony, dorsal and ventral surfaces are

fully flaked. The right lateral margin is slightly convex and thick with steep blunting; the left lateral margin is thin and shows minute retouch, which forms a point at the distal end with the arch, fresh.

14. Lunate on thin broad blade of jasper. Dorsal surface shows two forked longitudinal ridges, ventral surface shows primary flake surface. The arc is convex with minute steep blunting and the chord is straight and shows use-marks, fresh.

15. Lunate on thick blade of Chalcedony. Dorsal surface shows two longitudinal parallel ridges, ventral surface shows primary flake surface with the traces of a bulb. The arc is thick and convex and shows excellent blunting while the chord is thin and shows use-marks, fresh.

16. Asymmetrical triangle on a thick broad blade of Chalcedony. Dorsal surface shows a longitudinal ridge with shallow and deep flake scars. Ventral surface shows primary flake surface. The arc is thick and with two asymmetrical margins joins at the centre. Chord is straight and shows occasional use-marks, fresh.

17. Slightly broken parallel-sided blade of Chalcedony, dorsal surface shows a median high ridge with small shallow and deep flake scars on the right half of the tool. Ventral surface shows primary flake surface with a prominent bulb of percussion. The left lateral margin is minutely retouched, fresh.

18. Thin broad blade of Chalcedony, dorsal surface shows forked longitudinal ridge with small shallow and deep flake scars, ventral surface shows removal of the bulb and ripple marks. One of the margins is minutely retouched and the other shows use-marks, fresh.

19. A thick and broad blade of Chalcedony, dorsal surface shows three parallel-sided ridges with shallow and deep flake scars. Ventral surface shows primary flake surface with a prominent bulb of percussion and a facetted-striking platform. The lateral margin shows occasional use-marks.

20. A thick blade of Chalcedony with straight and slightly convex lateral margins, dorsal surface shows a forked high longitudinal ridge, with shallow and deep flake scars, and with longitudinal patch of cortex on the right half. Ventral surface shows primary flake surface with traces of a bulb. The lateral margin shows occasional use marks.

21. A narrow thick blade of jasper, slightly broken. The dorsal surface shows two longitudinal ridges with a patch of cortex. Ventral surface shows primary flake surface without traces of bulb, fresh.

22. A leaf shaped end flake of jasper, dorsal surface shows a forked longitudinal ridge. Ventral surface shows a primary flake surface with a bulb and prepared striking platform. Lateral margin shows use-marks.

23. A pointed flake of Chalcedony, dorsal surface shows a longitudinal median high ridge forked at the proximal end, ventral surface is primary with a prominent bulb of percussion and a bulbar scar with a facetted striking platform. Occasional use-marks are seen on left lateral margin, fresh.

24. A small rectangular fluted core on Chalcedony, the parallel-sided flutations with prepared striking platform on one end are visible on one of the faces and with the cortex on the other three sides, fresh.

25. Residual conical fluted core of Chalcedony, parallel sided and irregular flutations are seen all around its body with striking plat form on broad end, fresh.

26. Rectangular fluted core on Chalcedony with a prepared striking platform on one end. Parallel sided and irregular flutations on parts of its body, the remaining part of the body is with cortex, fresh.

REFERENCES

Sheshadri, M.	1953	Microlithic Industries of Mysore, Arluta, 9.
-	1954	Microlithic Industries of Kibbanahalli, Mysore State, C. S. XXIII
-	1956	*The Stone Using Cultures of Prehistoric and Protohistoric Mysore,* London.
Mallik, S. C.	1956 –57	*Indian Archaeology*—A Review.
Mishra, V. N.	1977	*Prehistoric Man and His Art in Central India.*
Madhusudhana Rao	1979	Stone Age Cultures of Paleru Valley, Prakasam District Andhra Pradesh, Ph.D.,Thesis, Nagarjuna University.
Kasturi Bai, M.	1982	The stone age cultures of Yeluru valley in East Godavari District, Andhra Pradesh, Ph.D., Thesis, Nagarjuna University.
Paddaiah, K.	1968	*Pre and Protohistoric Investigations in Shorapur Doab,* Ph.D., Unpublished Thesis, Poona University.
-	1970	The Blade Tool Industry of Shorapur, Doab, Peninsular, India, *I. A.* 4.
-	1974	Pre and Protohistoric Finds from Salvadgi Hills, Bijappor District, Karnataka, *Journal of the University of Poona,* (Humanities Section) 41.

Pappu, R. S. 1966 *Pleistocene Studies in Upper Krishna Basin.* Ph.D. Thesis Deccan College.

Raman K. V. 1960-61 *IAR,* 1960-61

Rajguru, S. N. & Hegde, K. T. M. 1972 The Pleistocene Stratigraphy in India, *Archaeological, Congress and Seminar Papers* (Ed. S. B. Deo) Nagpur, 74.

Rajguru, S. N. 1973 Pleistocene climatic changes in Western India, Radio Carbon and Indian Archaeology (Eds. D. B. Agarwal, A. Ghosh)

Rikes, R. 1967 *Water, Weather and Prehistory;* London.

Rami Reddy, V. 1968 *Pre and Protohistory of South Westren Andhra Pradesh,* Ph. D., Unpublished Thesis, Poona.

\- 1975 The Mesolithic Cultures in Kurnool and Ananthpur Districts, South India, *The Journal of the Karnataka University.*

Rami Reddy, V. 1976 The Prehistoric and Protohistoric Cultures of Palvoy, South India.

Sankalia, H. D. 1956 the Microlithic Industry of Langhnaj, in Gujarat Middle Stone Age Culture.

1963 In India and pakistan, *Science No. 146.* Excavations at Langhnaj 1944-63.

\- 1969 Mesolithic and Pre-Mesolithic Industry from the excavation at Sanganakallu, Bellary, 1965, Deccan College, Poona.

\- 1974 *Prehistory and Protohistory of India and Pakistan.*

Sharma, M. J. 1982 *The Upper Palaeolithic Culture of India,* Agamkala Prakasan, Delhi.

Soundara Rajan, K. V. 1950 Stone Age Industries Near Giddalur, District Kurnool, A. I. No. 8.

\- 1958 Studies in Stone Ages of Nagarjuna Konda and Its Neighbourhood A.I. 14.

Rao, S. N. 1966 *Stone Age Cultures of Nalgonda* Ph.D, Unpublished Thesis, Poona University, Deccan College Libraries.

Sali, S. A.	1970	IA 4
	1974	Upper Palaeolithic Researchers Since 1980, Independence, *Bulletin of the Deccan College,* 34.
	1980	*Stone Age Culture Sequence at Patne,* District Jalgaon, Maharashtra, Ph.D. Thesis, University of Poona.
Sharma, G. R.	1956-57	IAR pp 11-15.
	1964-65	-
	1973	Mesolithic Cultures in the Ganga Valley India, Proceeding of the Prehistoric Society, 39.
	1975	Seasonal Migrations and Mesolithic Lake Culture of the Ganga Valley, *Presidential Address, Indian Prehistoric Society,* Delhi.
-	1980	Archaeology of the Ganga Valley, History to Prehistory.
Vita Fing	1971	Heridity and Environment in Plastic Sediments: Silt/Clay Depletion, Geological Society of America, Bulletin, 82.
Vidula Jaiswal,	-	Palaeohistory of India
-	1973	*Study of the Prepared Core Technics in Palaeolithic Cultures of India,* Thesis, Banaras Hindu University.
Wain Wright, C.A.	1964	*The Pleistocene Deposit of the Lower Narmada River and an Early Stone Age India from the river Chambal,* Baroda.
Zeuner , F. E. & Allchin, B.		Microlithic Sites in Tinnelvalley District, Madras State, AI, 12

Selected Bibliography

ANDERSON, C. W. 1917 Notes on Prehistoric Implements Found in The Singhbhum District, JBORS, 3 : 349-362.

ANSARI, Z. D. & NAGARAJA RAO, M. S. 1969 Excavations at Sanganakallu, (1964-65) Deccan College, Poona.

BORDES, FRACOISE, 1968 The Old Stone Age, World University Library, London.

BROWN, COGGIN, 1917 Catalogue of Prehistoric Antiquities in The Indian Museum at Calcutta, Simla.

BURKITT, M. C. 1963 The Old Stone Age–A study of Palaeolithic Times.

COMMAIDE, L. A. 1924 Pygmy Implements of the Lower Godavari, *Man in India* 4: 83-105

COMMAIDE, L. A. & BURKITT, M. C. 1930 Fresh Light on the Stone Age of South East India, Antiquity, 4 : 327-339.

DANI, A. H. 1960 *Prehistory and Protohistory of Eastern India,* Calcutta.

FOOTE, R. B. 1866 On the occurrence of Stone implements in Various Parts of Madras and North Arcot Districts, MOLS, III Series.

1914 The Foote's Collection of Indian Prehistoric Antiquities, Madras.

1915 The Foote Collection of Indian Prehistoric and Protohistoric Antiquities – Notes on their Ages and Distribution, Madras.

GHOSH, A. 1948 Prehistoric Explorations in India, IHC 24(1) 1-18.

GORDAN, D. H. 1950 The Stone Industries of the Holocene in India and Pakistan, Ancient India 6: 64-90.

ISAAC, N. 1960 The Stone Age Cultures of Kurnool, Ph.D.

Unpublished Thesis, Poona University and Deccan College Libraries.

JOSHI, R. V. 1978 Stone Age Cultures of Central India, Deccan College, Post Graduate and Research Institute, Poona.

KHATRI, A. P. 1961 Stone Age and Pleistocene Chronology of The Narmada Valley, (Central India), *Anthronos,* 56 : 519–530.

KRISHNASWAMI, V. D. 1947 Stone Age in India, AI. 3 : 11–57.

1952 Progress in Prehistory, AI. 9: 53–79.

KRISHNASWAMI, V. D. & SOUNDARA RAJAN, K. V. 1951 The Lithic Tool-Industries of the Singrauli Basin, District Mirzapur, AI, 7: 40–65.

LYDEKKER, R. 1886 (a) Preliminary Note on the Mammalia of Kurnool Caves RGSI 19 : 2.

1886 (b) The Fauna of Kurnool Caves, Palasontolonis India, Series X4 : 2 : 22–58.

MALTI NAGAR 1975 Role of Ethnographic Evidence in the Reconstruction of Archaeological data, *The Eastern Anthropologist,* 28 (1) : 13–22.

MISHRA, V. N. 1962 Problems of terminology in Indian Pre-History, Eastern Anthropologist, 15 (2) : 113–124.

MISHRA, V. N. 1967 Pre- and Protohistory of the Berach Basin South Rajasthan, Deccan College, Poona.

MISHRA, V. N. & M. NAGAR 1973 Twenty-five years of Indian Prehistory (1947–1972) a Review of research, in *Man and Society,* Lucknow, Ed. By K.S. Mathur : 1-54.

MISHRA, V. N. 1973 Bagor a Late Mesolithic Settlement in North-West India, *World Archaeology,* 5(1) : 92 :110.

MOONE, H. V. V. 1934 A Classification of Flint Burins or Gravers, PPSLXIV : 81–92.

MUTTON, JH. 1928 Prehistory of Assam, Man in India, 88 : 228–229.

NAIDU, A. S. 1966 Lithological and Chemical Facies Changes in the Recent Deltaic Sediments of the Godavari River,

India; 'Deltas' in their Geologic frame-work published by Houston Geological Society, U.S.A.

PADDAIAH, K 1974 Pre-and-Protohistoric finds from Salvadgi Hills, Bijapur, District, Karnataka, *Journal of the University of Poona,* (Humanities Section) 41 : 109-43.

RAJAGURU, S. N. 1973 On the Problem of Late Pleistocene's Climate changes in Western Maharashtra, in *Radio Carbon and Indian Archaeology,* Ed. D.P. Agrawal and A. Ghosh, Bombay, 80-84.

1981 Problems of Late Pleistocene Aridity in India, VIII Indian Society for Pre-Historic and Quaternary Studies.

RAMI REDDY, V. 1968 *Pre- and Protohistory of South Western Andhra Pradesh,* Ph.D., Unpublished Thesis, Poona Libraries.

SANKALIA, H. D. 1956 *The Microlithic Industry of Langhnai,* Gujarat.

1964 *Stone Age Tools, Their Techniques, Names And Probable Functions,* Deccan College, Poona.

1965 Excavations at Langhnai, 1944-63, Part I, Archaeology, Poona.

SHESHADRI, M. 1953 Microlithic Industries of Mysore, Arluta, 9 : 29–38

1954 Microlithic Industries Kibbanahalli, Mysore State CS. XXIII : 326-7

1956 *The Stone Using cultures of Prehistoric And Protohistoric Mysore,* London.

SHARMA G. R. 1973 Mesolithic cultures in Ganga valley, India, Proceedings of the Prehistoric Society, 39 : 129-46.

SHARAM T. C. 1974 Recent Archaeological Discoveries in North Eastern India, *Puratattva,* 7 : 17-19.

SMITH, V. 1906 Pigmy implements, Indian Antiquary, 35 : 185–96.

SUBBA RAO, B. 1948 *Stone age Cultures of Bellary,* Poona.

SUBRAHMANYAM, B. R. — *Excavation of Jami. Visakhapatnam District* (In Press) 'Prehistory' Chapter II in *Comprehensive History of Andhra Pradesh* (In Press).

VARMA, R. K. 1974 The Upper Palaeolithic Industry of the Belan Valley paper read in the Symposium Of Indian Prehistory 1974, Organised by the Deccan College, Pune (Un-Published).

★★★

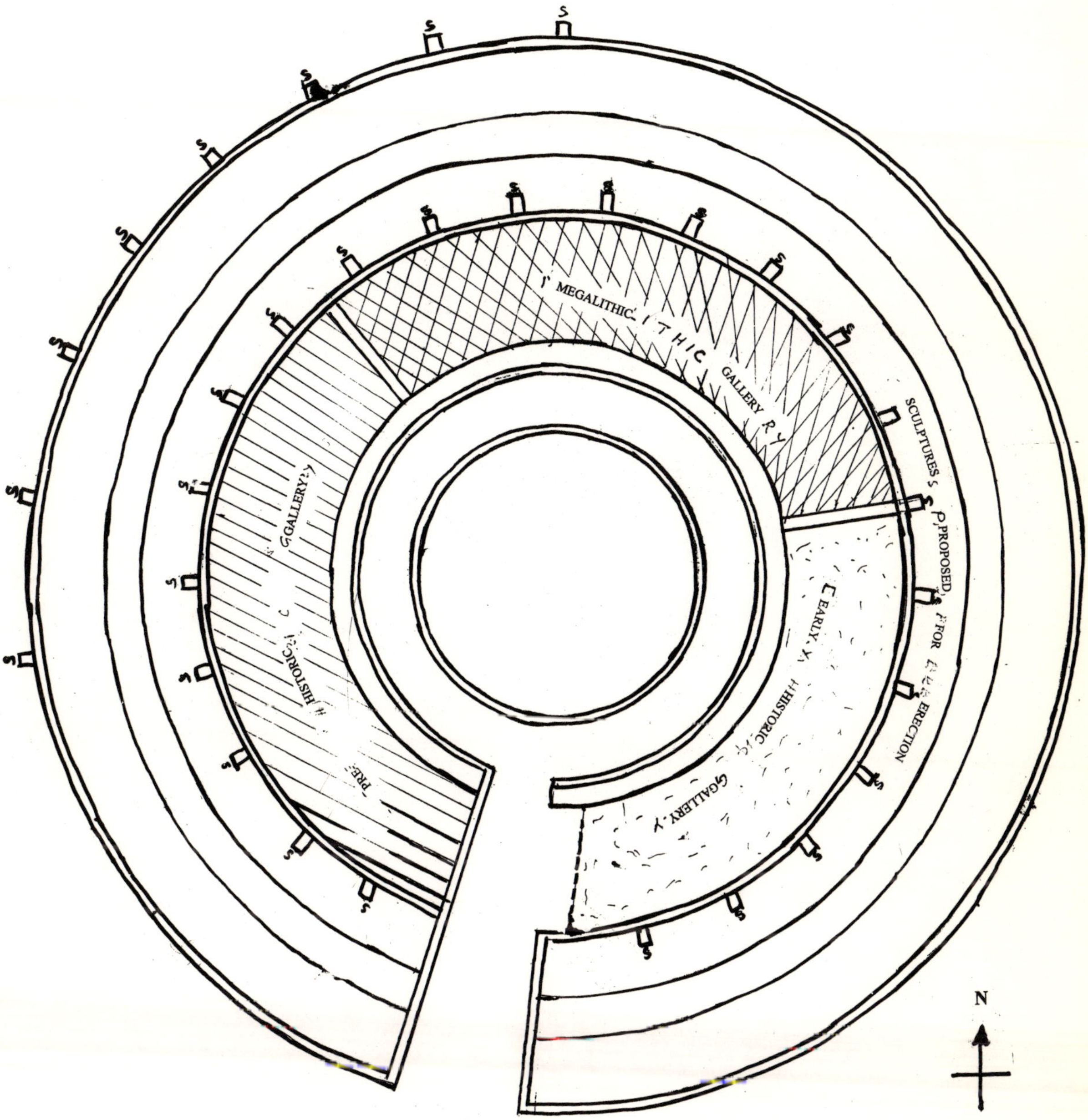

FIG. I—CIRCULAR PLAN OF SRISAILAM PAVILION AREA OF DISPLAY OF PRE-HISTORIC TOOLS.

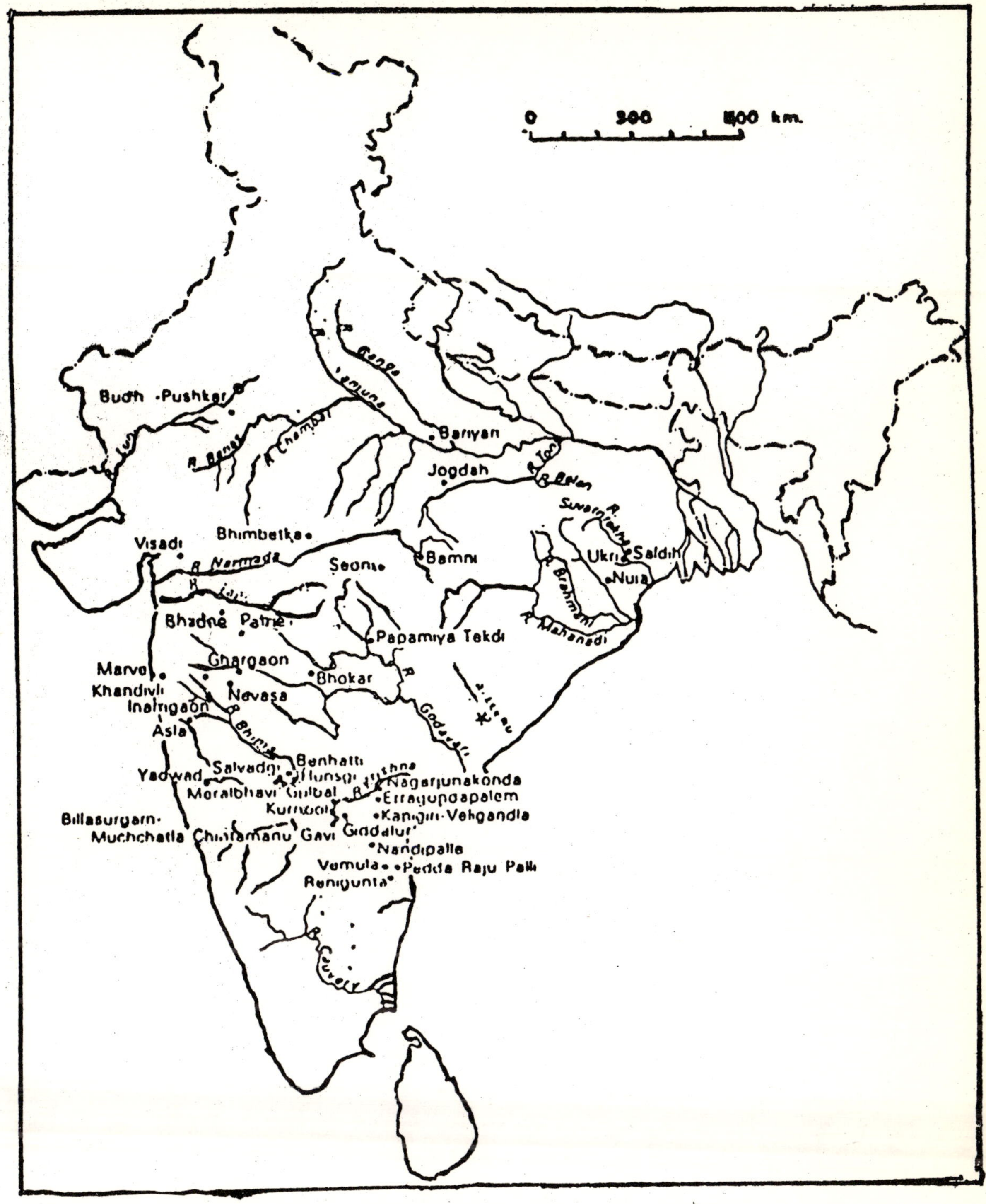

FIG. II—MAP SHOWING IMPORTANT UPPER PALAEOLITHIC SITES IN INDIA.

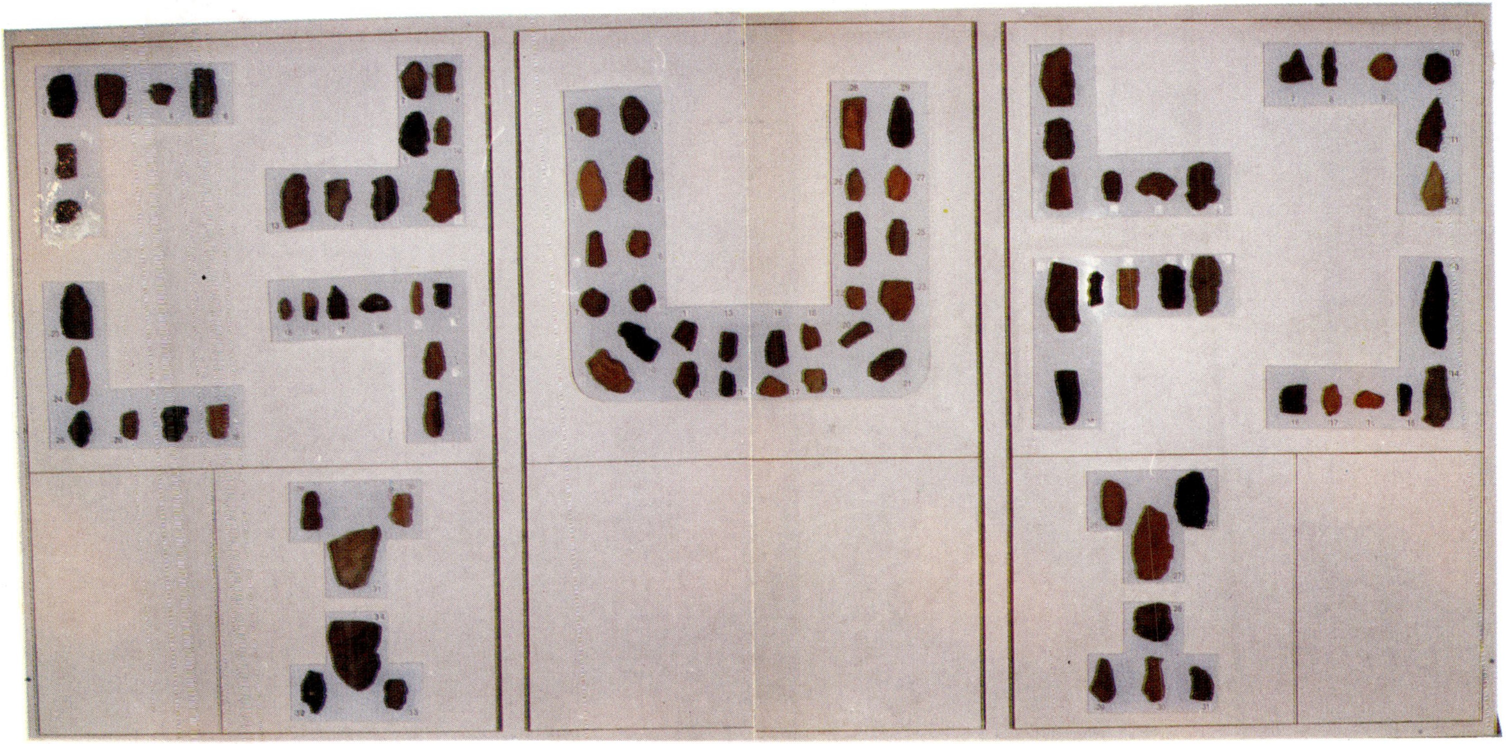

PL. XIII. Tool Assemblage of Upper Palaeolithic Period

PL. XIV. Tool Types Found In Different Sites in Andhra Pradesh–
Upper Palaeolithic Period

PL. XI. Tools Showing Diversified Activity–Middle Palaeolithic Period

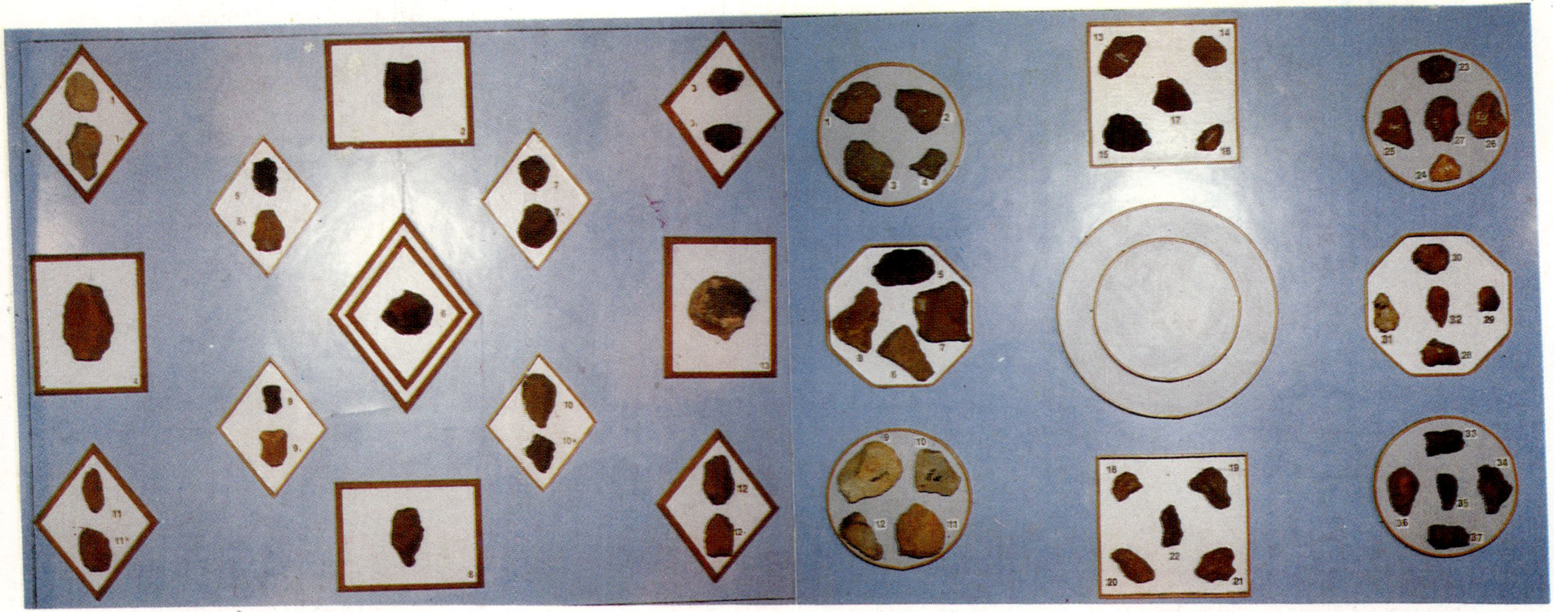

PL. XII. Standardized Tool Types of Various Sites Found in Andhra Pradesh–Middle Palaeolithic Period

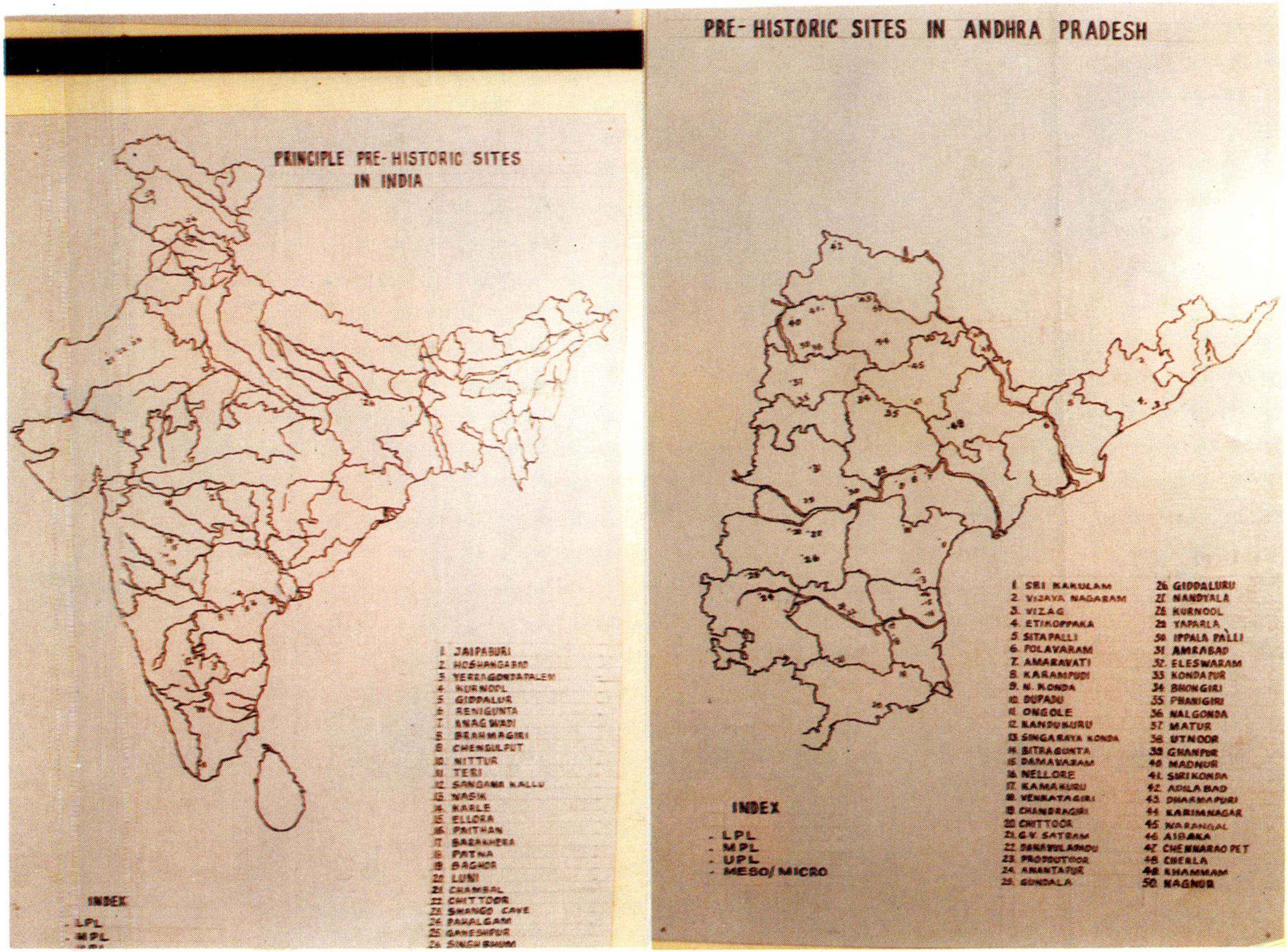

PL. XV. Maps Showing Distribution of Prehistoric Sites

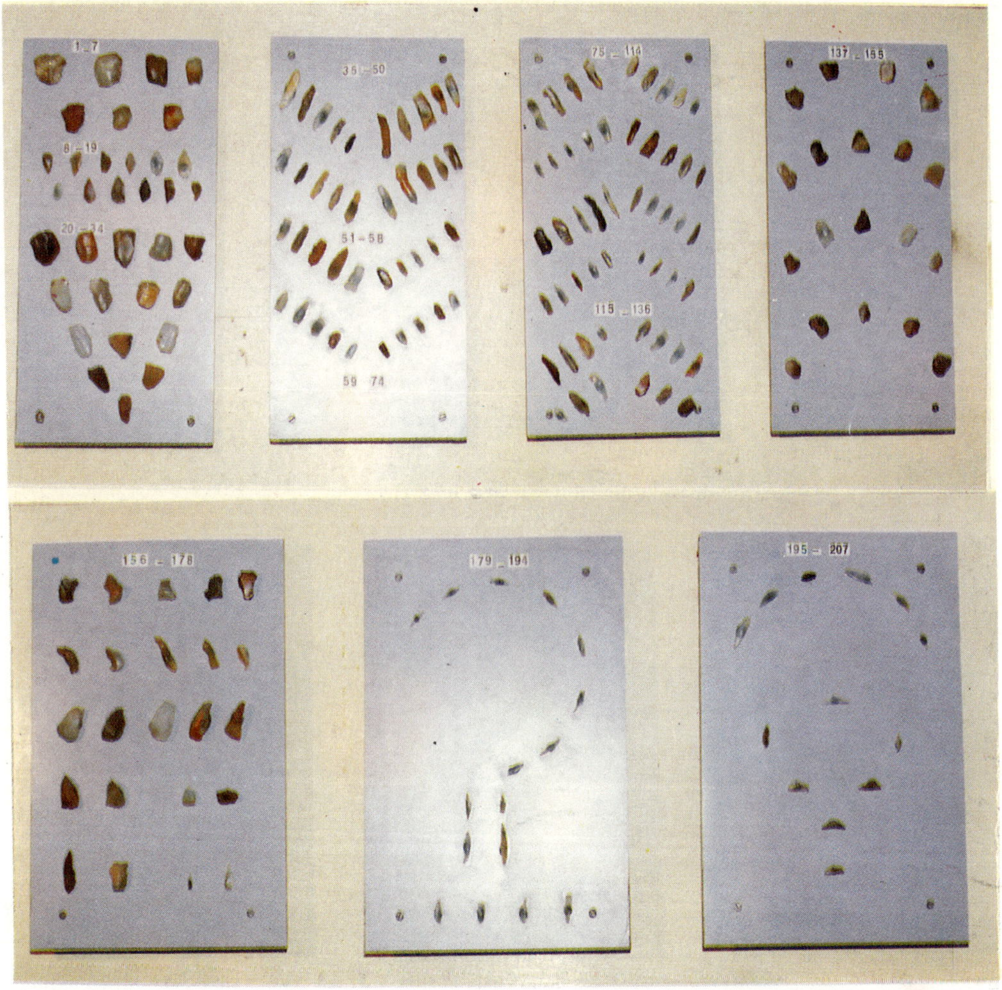

PL. XVI. Tool Types of the Mesolithic Period